God's
MODEL
of
FORGIVENESS

God's
MODEL
of
FORGIVENESS

How You Can Model
God's Forgiveness

KEVIN MADISON

ISBN: Paperback 979-8-9876047-0-0
ISBN: Ebook 979-8-9876047-2-4

Design and publishing assistance by The Happy Self-Publisher.

To my mother, Billie Mae Phillips, who loves me and encourages me daily to follow Christ Jesus, the King of Glory, with all my heart. One day, mother, I will stand next to you before the Judgment Seat of Christ as He hands out your reward for bringing members of your family with you to heaven. What a glorious day that will be!

TABLE OF CONTENTS

Introduction ix

The Introduction 1

The Backstory 7

The Relationship 17

The Character of Forgiveness 23

The Walk of Forgiveness 43

The Motive of Forgiveness 69

Bibliography 91

About the Author 93

INTRODUCTION

*A*h life, sometimes it seems to be so trivial, so fickle: long seasons of pain, sorrows, and sufferings; short seasons of happiness, fulfillment, and satisfaction, the revolving ebbs and flow of life in pursuit of the unobtainable.

The Lord God offers all people everlasting fulfillment where love, joy, and peace abide forever. This hope is not found in a place or a possession. It is only found in one person, Jesus Christ, the Son of the Most High God. For those willing to repent of their sins and believe in Jesus, God will give them true satisfaction that not even death can take away.

FORGIVENESS!

[1] Blessed is he whose transgression is forgiven, whose sin is covered. [2] Blessed is the man to whom the LORD does not impute iniquity, and in whose spirit there is no deceit. **Psalms 32:1-2**

THE
INTRODUCTION

*W*ho was Philemon? Scriptures tell us that he was a prominent member of the church at Colossea (**vv. 1, 2; cf. Col. 4:9**), which met in his house (**v. 2**). The letter was for him, his family, and the church.

Philemon had been saved under Paul's ministry, most likely during the time Paul was ministering in Ephesus (**v. 19**), a few years prior to the writing of this letter. In a general reading of the letter's contents, it appears that Philemon's family was wealthy enough to have a large house (**cf. v. 2**), owned at least one slave, a man named Onesimus (literally "useful"; a common name for slaves). However, it was very common during those times that the wealthy owned many slaves to perform tasks. Men in those days worked off their debts by submitting themselves to be slaves to the wealthy, not employees. They had no rights, were often treated with disdain, and lived in horrible conditions. Of course, one would find a man who treated his slaves like family, but they were few and far between. The Roman culture did not look favorably upon slaves or servants. Therefore, this attitude was prevalent throughout the empire. Hence, the residents in each province often behaved like Roman citizens, which some were.

Onesimus, who was one of Philemon's slaves, was not a believer in Christ at the time he stole some money **(v. 18)** from Philemon and ran away. This action taken by Onesimus was also typical due to the harsh conditions and a very difficult life of servitude. Therefore, like countless thousands of other runaway slaves, Onesimus fled to Rome. In this very large metropolis, Onesimus sought to hide himself in the imperial capital's swarming and nondescript slave population. Somehow, miraculously, or shall we state, through the providence of God, through circumstances not recorded in scripture, Onesimus met Paul in Rome.

Was Paul in jail when he met Onesimus? It appears that Paul was, as evidenced by his statement, "Whom I have begotten while in my chains." The question is, Why was Onesimus in jail? Was he there as a prisoner? I doubt it based on the letter. Was he there working? Most likely, as it wouldn't be a place where someone would typically look for an employed criminal wanted for theft and abandonment, for which the penalty in the Roman Empire was death.

Yet, in these horrible conditions for both Paul and Onesimus, the providence of the Lord was at work. Onesimus was counted among the elect "before the foundation of the world." One may ask the question, Are you stating that God had Onesimus become a slave, encouraged him to steal and run away to Rome to meet Paul in prison? Kevin, that's just too much.

No, my friend. That's not what I am stating at all, and that would not be a biblical perspective on the providence of the Almighty. God is holy, therefore, is incapable of "causing" or "enticing" anyone to sin in any way. What I am stating is that God used Onesimus' rebellion to preach the gospel to him through Paul. God prepared Paul to share the gospel and prepared Onesimus' heart to receive the gospel.

One may then inquire, Well, wasn't Philemon a Christian? Couldn't he or other members of the church at Colossea preach the gospel to Onesimus? Of course, they could have, and maybe they did. The scriptures doesn't state either way, and there is no benefit for us to speculate. What we know factually from the letter's content is that Philemon may not have been treating his slaves like the Lord would have him treat them. Paul had to admonish Philemon to treat Onesimus as a brother and others as servants. Either way, God prepared both Paul and Onesimus that salvation would come to Onesimus, the bond between Paul and Philemon would grow stronger, repentance and restitution from Onesimus, forgiveness and reconciliation from Philemon, reconciliation between Philemon and Onesimus, and the bond of brotherly love between all three men. Oh, the glory of being in Christ who was made sin, who knew no sin, who reconciled us to God through His precious blood, burial, and resurrection. All glory, honor, majesty, power, and dominion be unto You, O Lord God, our Heavenly Father, Lord, and King. We worship and praise Your wonderful name both now and forever. Amen.

We also note that Paul quickly grew to love the runaway slave (**vv. 12, 16**) and desired to keep Onesimus in Rome (**v. 13**), where he was providing valuable service to Paul in his imprisonment (**v. 11**). Apparently, Onesimus was Paul's channel of communication to the churches. Most likely, he tended to Paul's needs as well by bringing food and clothing offered by the churches.

As the fellowship and trust between Paul and Onesimus grew, Paul discovered through conversation not revelation who Onesimus was and what he had done. What a shock it must have been to Paul to hear that Onesimus was a slave under Philemon. No, not the fact that Onesimus was a slave, there were millions of slaves in the Roman Empire and even among the Jews. This was normal. Therefore, no one would have objected or been surprised by that part of the confession. Now this isn't to condone slavery in any way but stating the factual truth isn't an option with God or His servants, the true believers in Christ. Armed with this knowledge was both a surprise and relief to Paul because of his long-term relationship with Philemon. Therefore, Paul, through the wisdom of the Holy Spirit, understood the importance of reconciliation between Philemon and Onesimus. Though he desired that Onesimus remain in Rome to continue to serve with him in the ministry, the word of God must be honored. Therefore, Paul pushed his desire aside in order that Christ would be glorified.

Note that Paul could have used the excuse that since the word of God is being preached, the ministry is growing, people are being saved, and all evidence abounds that God is lovingly blessing the ministry. To the contrary of all the external evidence, God would not be pleased with or glorified through Paul if he had not fully obeyed the Word of God by sending Onesimus back to Philemon to be held accountable for the sinful actions he took. It doesn't matter that Onesimus was not a Christian, a true disciple of Jesus Christ. Even with Christians, God's words and natural moral laws are immutable. Everyone reaps whatever they sow if we Christians sow to our flesh, we Christians will reap corruption. One can say that you don't believe in the law of gravity, but I would not challenge it by stepping off a 30-story building.

Nonetheless, by stealing and abandoning his master, Philemon, Onesimus had both broken Roman law and defrauded his master. Paul knew, according to the commandments of our Lord, that those issues had to be dealt with, and decided to send Onesimus back to Colossea. Think of the conversation that took place between Paul and Onesimus. One day they are rejoicing in the Lord; the next day,

Paul is saying, Onesimus, you must go home and right the wrongs you have with Philemon. Christ cannot use you while you persist in this sin. I know you think you are free and in this physical life you are. However, don't give place to the devil to ensnare you by not being obedient to God. Go home and face the consequences of your sinful actions. I know Philemon and will beg for leniency on your behalf. Peradventure the Lord will show us both mercy and kindness.

Since it was too hazardous for Onesimus to make the trip alone due to the presence of runaway slavecatchers, Paul decided to send him back with Tychicus, who was returning to Colossea with the epistle to the Colossians (**Col. 4:7–9**). Along with Onesimus, Paul sent Philemon this beautiful personal letter, graciously pleading and urging him to forgive Onesimus and welcome him back to service as a brother in Christ not a mere slave, which Onesimus, in actuality, was. (**vv. 15–17**).

THE
BACKSTORY

*I*n this letter to Philemon, there are valuable historical intuitions into the first century church's relationship with respect to the governance and institution of slavery. One must understand that slavery was widespread throughout the Roman Empire and all the previous empires prior to Rome's conquest. According to historical estimates, slaves constituted one-third to one-half, of the population and slavery was an accepted part of life. In Paul's day, slavery had virtually eclipsed free labor and those of "low-born" status would sell their male offspring to the wealthy, who in turn would adopt some as heirs, especially if the "low-born" child of a slave was very athletic or intelligent.

Unlike our history and understanding of slavery, slaves during Paul's days in the Roman Empire could be professionals, such as doctors, musicians, teachers, artists, librarians, or accountants; in short, almost all jobs could be and were filled, in part, by slaves. Yet, these slaves were not legally considered persons, but were the tools of their masters. As such, they could be bought, sold, inherited, exchanged, or seized to pay their master's debt. Their masters had virtually unlimited power to punish them, and sometimes did so severely for the slightest infractions. Listen to

Abraham to Sarah concerning her Egyptian slave, Hagar: [5] Then Sarai said to Abram, "My wrong be upon you! I gave my maid into your embrace; and when she saw that she had conceived, I became despised in her eyes. The LORD judge between you and me." [6] So Abram said to Sarai, "**Indeed your maid is in your hand; do to her as you please.**" And when Sarai dealt harshly with her, she fled from her presence. **Genesis 16:5-6**

Does this mean that masters should treat their slaves inhumanely? Of course not. It was simply a means to convey how slavery was viewed in that period. Just because something is mentioned in the word of God, it doesn't mean that God approves of it. God is simply telling us what happened, stating the facts. Everything the Lord God approves is written to us as imperatives and commandments, leaving no doubt to the reader what God's desires, expectations, and demands are. These are not given to be questioned. They are instructions to be obeyed without reservation.

Like all human history, by the time of the New Testament, slavery, the implications, imperatives, and implementations were beginning to transition. The masters, recognizing that contented slaves were more productive, began to treat them more leniently. It was becoming common for a master to teach a slave the master's own trade; some masters and slaves became close friends. Although the Caesars of Rome never acknowledged them as persons under the law, the Roman Senate in A.D. 20 granted slaves accused of crimes the right to a trial. One advent that really changed the slave market and value was when slaves were granted their freedom, or someone could purchase their freedom. Those slaves who were of prominent houses enjoyed very favorable and profitable serviceable lifestyles under their masters and were much better off than many freemen and Roman citizens because they were guaranteed care and provision even for their offspring. Many, many, many freemen struggled in poverty and were destitute.

Nowhere in the word of God does it directly attack slavery. This falls under the permissive will of God through the wisdom of God. Why do I say such a thing? Because God knew and knows how desperately wicked the heart of man really is. Had He attacked slavery and commanded it to cease, it would have resulted in slave insurrections which would have been brutally suppressed, leading to the death of untold millions of slaves unable to protect themselves, and the message of the gospel hopelessly confused with that of social reform.

Please hear me well. God is not interested in social justice reforms! You may ask, Then what does God want?

God is a Savior. This is what the scriptures teach, and this is God's purpose: [23]Therefore, the One whom you worship without knowing, Him I proclaim to you: [24] God, who made the world and everything in it, since He is Lord of heaven and earth, does not dwell in temples made with hands. [25] Nor is He worshiped with men's hands, as though He needed anything, since He gives to all life, breath, and all things. [26] And He has made from one blood every nation of men to dwell on all the face of the earth, and has determined their preappointed times and the boundaries of their dwellings, [27] **so that they should seek the Lord, in the hope that they might grope for Him and find Him**, though He is not far from each one of us; [28] for in Him we live and move and have our being, as also some of your own poets have said, 'For we are also His offspring.' [29] Therefore, since we are the offspring of God, we ought not to think that the Divine Nature is like gold or silver or stone, something shaped by art and man's devising. [30] **Truly, these** times of ignorance God overlooked, but now commands all men everywhere to repent, [31] because He has appointed a day on which He will judge the world in righteousness by the Man whom He has ordained. He has given assurance of this to all by raising Him from the dead." Acts 17:23-31

Jesus gave us the definitive answer: [32] I have not come to call the righteous, but sinners, to repentance." Luke 5:32

[9] And Jesus said to him, "Today salvation has come to this house, because he also is a son of Abraham; [10] for the Son of Man has come to seek and to save that which was lost." Luke 19:9-10

In the infinite wisdom of our Creator, the Lord God undermined the evils of slavery, not by destroying the Roman Empire, replacing the Caesars, petitioning politicians, or revising the laws. No, none of that foolishness as laws in the hands of wicked, evil, ungodly unbelievers will never be honored. The Lord deals with slavery at its core, by changing the hearts of slaves and masters through repentance, reconciliation, and forgiveness.

The word of God placed the focus on the spiritual equality of master and slave.

[15] For perhaps he departed for a while for this purpose, that you might receive him forever, [16] no longer as a slave but more than a slave—a beloved brother, especially to me but how much more to you, both in the flesh and in the Lord. Philemon 1:15-16

[26] For you are all sons of God through faith in Christ Jesus. [27] For as many of you as were baptized into Christ have put on Christ. [28] There is neither Jew nor Greek, there is neither slave nor free, there is neither male nor female; for you are all one in Christ Jesus. Galatians 3:26-28

⁹ And you, masters, do the same things to them, giving up threatening, knowing that your own Master also is in heaven, and there is no partiality with Him. **Ephesians 6:9**

¹ Masters, give your bondservants what is just and fair, knowing that you also have a Master in heaven. **Colossians 4:1**

¹ Let as many bondservants as are under the yoke count their own masters worthy of all honor, so that the name of God and His doctrine may not be blasphemed. ² And those who have believing masters, let them not despise them because they are brethren, but rather serve them because those who are benefited are believers and beloved. Teach and exhort these things. **1 Timothy 6:1-2**

What was and is God's method of dealing with slavery? Salvation, which results in an overwhelming love for God and a love for the children of God.

⁷ Brethren, I write no new commandment to you, but an old commandment which you have had from the beginning. The old commandment is the word which you heard from the beginning. ⁸ Again, a new commandment I write to you, which thing is true in Him and in you, because the darkness is passing away, and the true light is already shining. ⁹ He who says he is in the light, and hates his brother, is in darkness until now. ¹⁰ He who loves his brother abides in the light, and there is no cause for stumbling in him. ¹¹ But he who hates his brother is in darkness and walks in darkness, and does not know where he is going, because the darkness has blinded his eyes. **1 John 2:7-11**

By changing slaves and masters from the inside, creating within each a new human spirit, through His abiding love and word, God did away with slavery's abuses.

These commands are given to each true believer in and through the love of God, which is in His Son, Christ Jesus the King of Glory. Every born-again true believer is hidden in Christ in God.

[1] If then you were raised with Christ, seek those things which are above, where Christ is, sitting at the right hand of God. [2] Set your mind on things above, not on things on the earth. [3] **For you died, and your life is hidden with Christ in God.** [4] When Christ who is our life appears, then you also will appear with Him in glory. **Colossians 3:1-4**

Note that that word "if" isn't the if of condition, meaning maybe you were or weren't raised with Christ. No, beloved, it's the "if" of argument meaning "since." It's an imperative fact of a definitive action previously taken by the Lord.

So, what are the commandments of love? They are:

1. The Imperative of Love

[10] In this the children of God and the children of the devil are manifest: Whoever does not practice righteousness is not of God, nor is he who does not love his brother. [11] For this is the message that you heard from the beginning, that we should love one another, [12] not as Cain who was of the wicked one and murdered his brother. And why did he murder him? Because his works were evil and his brother's righteous. [13] Do not marvel, my brethren, if the world hates you. [14] We know that we have passed from death to life, because we love the brethren. He who does not love his brother abides in death. [15] Whoever hates his brother is a murderer, and you know that no murderer has eternal life abiding in him. **1 John 3:10-15**

2. The Outworking of Love

¹⁶ By this we know love because He laid down His life for us. And we also ought to lay down our lives for the brethren. ¹⁷ But whoever has this world's goods, and sees his brother in need, and shuts up his heart from him, how does the love of God abide in him? ¹⁸ My little children, let us not love in word or in tongue, but in deed and in truth. ¹⁹ And by this we know that we are of the truth and shall assure our hearts before Him. ²⁰ For if our heart condemns us, God is greater than our heart, and knows all things. ²¹ Beloved, if our heart does not condemn us, we have confidence toward God. ²² And whatever we ask we receive from Him, because we keep His commandments and do those things that are pleasing in His sight. ²³ And this is His commandment: that we should believe on the name of His Son Jesus Christ and love one another, as He gave us commandment. **1 John 3:16-23**

3. Knowing God Through Love

⁷ Beloved, let us love one another, for love is of God; and everyone who loves is born of God and knows God. ⁸ He who does not love does not know God, for God is love. ⁹ In this the love of God was manifested toward us, that God has sent His only begotten Son into the world, that we might live through Him. ¹⁰ In this is love, not that we loved God, but that He loved us and sent His Son to be the propitiation for our sins. ¹¹ Beloved, if God so loved us, we also ought to love one another. **1 John 4:7-11**

4. Seeing God Through Love

¹² No one has seen God at any time. If we love one another, God abides in us, and His love has been perfected in us. ¹³ By

this we know that we abide in Him, and He in us, because He has given us of His Spirit. [14] And we have seen and testify that the Father has sent the Son as Savior of the world. [15] Whoever confesses that Jesus is the Son of God, God abides in him, and he in God. [16] And we have known and believed the love that God has for us. God is love, and he who abides in love abides in God, and God in him. **1 John 4:12-16**

5. The Consummation of Love

[17] Love has been perfected among us in this: that we may have boldness in the day of judgment; because as He is, so are we in this world. [18] There is no fear in love; but perfect love casts out fear, because fear involves torment. But he who fears has not been made perfect in love. [19] We love Him because He first loved us. **1 John 4:17-19**

6. Obedience by Faith in Love

[20] If someone says, "I love God," and hates his brother, he is a liar; for he who does not love his brother whom he has seen, how can he love God whom he has not seen? [21] And this commandment we have from Him: that he who loves God must love his brother also. [1] Whoever believes that Jesus is the Christ is born of God, and everyone who loves Him who begot also loves him who is begotten of Him. [2] By this we know that we love the children of God, when we love God and keep His commandments. [3] For this is the love of God, that we keep His commandments. And His commandments are not burdensome. [4] For whatever is born of God overcomes the world. And this is the victory that has overcome the world—our faith. [5] Who is he who overcomes the world, but he who believes that Jesus is the Son of God? **1 John 4:20 - 5:5**

The powerful doctrinal theme that alone permeates this letter is forgiveness, which happens to be one of the featured themes throughout New Testament scripture as it is central to the message of the gospel of Christ.

⁴ And forgive us our sins, for we also forgive everyone who is indebted (in sins) to us. And do not lead us into temptation but deliver us from the evil one." **Luke 11:4**

³² And be kind to one another, tenderhearted, forgiving one another, even **as God in Christ forgave you. Ephesians 4:32**

¹² Therefore, as the elect of God, holy and beloved, put on tender mercies, kindness, humility, meekness, longsuffering; ¹³ bearing with one another, and **forgiving one another, if anyone has a complaint against another; even as Christ forgave you, so you also must do**. ¹⁴ But above all these things put on love, which is the bond of perfection. ¹⁵ And let the peace of God rule in your hearts, to which also you were called in one body; and be thankful. **Colossians 3:12-15**

The Holy Spirit puts God the Father, Christ, and the sinner fully on display as Paul's instruction to Philemon provides the biblical definition of forgiveness, without ever using the word.

³³ Oh, the depth of the riches both of the wisdom and knowledge of God! How unsearchable are His judgments and His ways past finding out! ³⁴ "For who has known the mind of the LORD? Or who has become His counselor?" ³⁵ "Or who has first given to Him and it shall be repaid to him?" ³⁶ For of Him and through Him and to Him are all things, to whom be glory forever. Amen. **Romans 11:33-36**

THE
RELATIONSHIP

*I*sn't it interesting that the Lord would include a letter in the word of God to an owner of slaves, about a runaway slave. I wonder how many people recognize this truth. The scriptures actually engage this topic in several books of the Bible and has extensive instructions on the ownership of slaves and not necessarily in a negative light. It provides the who, the treatment, and the duration that people can be slaves.

The first mention of slaves, mostly noted as servants due to the translators' political correctness, is found in Genesis and continues throughout the Old Testament. The Lord God permitted slavery even among His people in Israel. What was forbidden was remaining a slave beyond 49 years. After seven sabbatical years, on the tenth day of the seventh month; on the Day of Atonement all debt including slaves were to be forgiven and released from bondage. This fiftieth year signified the year of Jubilee. The seven sabbatical years are for God, signifying the completion of atonement for sins. On the same day that the Lamb of God is sacrificed, freedom is pronounced upon all who believe.

The Year of Jubilee

[8] 'And you shall count seven sabbaths of years for yourself, seven times seven years; and the time of the seven sabbaths of years shall be to you forty-nine years. [9] Then you shall cause the trumpet of the Jubilee to sound on the tenth day of the seventh month; on the Day of Atonement you shall make the trumpet to sound throughout all your land. [10] And you shall consecrate the fiftieth year, and proclaim liberty throughout all the land to all its inhabitants. It shall be a Jubilee for you; and each of you shall return to his possession, and each of you shall return to his family. [11] That fiftieth year shall be a Jubilee to you; in it, you shall neither sow nor reap what grows of its own accord, nor gather the grapes of your untended vine. [12] For it is the Jubilee; it shall be holy to you; you shall eat its produce from the field. [13] In this Year of Jubilee, each of you shall return to his possession. [14] And if you sell anything to your neighbor or buy from your neighbor's hand, you shall not oppress one another. [15] According to the number of years after the Jubilee you shall buy from your neighbor, and according to the number of years of crops he shall sell to you. [16] According to the multitude of years you shall increase its price, and according to the fewer number of years you shall diminish its price; for he sells to you according to the number of the years of the crops. [17] Therefore you shall not oppress one another, but you shall fear your God; for I am the LORD your God. **Leviticus 25:8-17**

For Israel, this marked the return of the Jewish Messiah to free all the slaves of sin, destroy all the enemies of the Jewish nation, to be seated upon the throne of David in Jerusalem, and to be crowned King of kings and Lord of lords.

With all humanity sold under sin by our earthly father, Adam, all are born slaves to sin. Upon being redeemed by faith in Christ, the newly created human spirit is now a slave to righteousness and Christ. We are not our own. We were purchased with the precious blood of Christ, who alone is without blemish and without spot.

[19] Or do you not know that **your body is the temple of the Holy Spirit** who is in you, whom you have from God, and **you are not your own?** [20] For **you were bought at a price;** therefore glorify God in your body and in your spirit, which are God's. **1 Corinthians 6:19-20**

[18] knowing that **you were not redeemed with corruptible things**, like silver or gold, from your aimless conduct received by tradition from your fathers, [19] **but with the precious blood of Christ**, as of a lamb without blemish and without spot. [20] He indeed was foreordained before the foundation of the world, but was manifest in these last times for you [21] who through Him believe in God, who raised Him from the dead and gave Him glory, **so that your faith and hope are in God. 1 Peter 1:18-21**

We are now slaves of righteousness, free from the total control and condemnation of sin.

Before we traverse into our verse-by-verse study of Philemon, let me remind you that slavery is not prohibited in the word of God. It is merged into a brotherly love and respectful relationship from the new heart given by the Lord. The master and the slave are on equal footing before the throne of Christ. The word of God does condemn any form of abuse, in particular with the master abusing the slaves. This is the same relationship that governs employers and employees in Christ. The Christian relationship governs the family and work relationships.

The book of Philemon primarily deals with forgiveness of someone who hurt you deeply.

Here is the outline:

1. Paul's Salutation to and Blessing upon Philemon Verses 1 through 3
2. The Character of Forgiveness – Verses 4 through 7
3. The Walk of Forgiveness – Verses 8 through 18
4. The Motives of Forgiveness – Verses 19 through 25

Verse 1

[1] Paul, a prisoner of Christ Jesus, and Timothy our brother, to Philemon our beloved friend and fellow laborer, **Philemon 1:1**

It is not ironic that the Holy Spirit led Paul to write this epistle while he was in a Roman prison awaiting trial for preaching the gospel of Jesus Christ. Although Paul was confined as a prisoner of Caesar Nero, he was actually there by divine appointment.

[12] But I want you to know, brethren, **that the things which happened to me have actually turned out for the furtherance of the gospel**, [13] so that it has become evident to the whole palace guard, and to all the rest, that my chains are in Christ; [14] and most of the brethren in the Lord, having become confident by my chains, are much more bold to speak the word without fear. **Philippians 1:12-14**

Let this be a reminder to you, beloved, that not all negative events that happens in our lives are the results of chastisement from the Lord or hinderance by the enemy. This is the same lesson that Joseph confessed to his brothers.

[20] But as for you, you meant evil against me; but God meant it for good, in order to bring it about as it is this day, to save many people alive. **Genesis 50:20**

Caesar, as our Lord told Pontius Pilot, had no power over Paul unless it was given unto him by our Heavenly Father.

Paul truly considered himself a slave to Christ and His righteousness. Next, Paul mentions his son in the faith, Timothy, of whom Paul remarked elsewhere in the scriptures that none was more faithful to the cause and to him like Timothy. Oh, to have a friend like that who is also a brother in Christ.

The letter was written directly to Philemon who was known as a man of means and a generous person. He allowed the church to meet in his home. Remember, most members of the early church were poor and slaves who had to meet at the end of a hard day's work. Yes, there were some members who had more than a day's means, but most worked to eat that day.

Not only was Philemon a friend who came to the Lord through the ministry of Paul while he was in Ephesus, but a fellow laborer. Paul is referring to the work being conducted in the kingdom of God.

Verse 2
² to the beloved Apphia, Archippus our fellow soldier, and to the church in your house: **Philemon 1:2**

Paul then greets Apphia, Philemon's wife, who happens to be a believer and then their son, Archippus. Note the commendation given to Archippus as a fellow soldier of the Lord who called him to the ministry. Finally, Paul greets the entire Colossian church that met in Philemon's house.

Verse 3
³ Grace to you and peace from God our Father and the Lord Jesus Christ. **Philemon 1:3**

Note the order, grace then peace. No one can expect to have peace with God until they have been saved by the grace of God. Isaiah had this to say about God's peace:

[22] "There is no peace," says the LORD, "for the wicked." **Isaiah 48:22,**

and just in case we didn't get it the first time, God says it again.

[21] "There is no peace," Says my God, "for the wicked." **Isaiah 57:21**

THE CHARACTER OF FORGIVENESS

Verse 4

⁴ I thank my God, making mention of you always in my prayers, **Philemon 1:4**

In this verse, we find the classic example of the evidence of saving faith.

1. Thankfulness "I thank"
2. A reverence and acknowledgment of God "my God" – it's personal
3. Love for fellow believers "making mention of you"
4. A strong desire for them to follow and obey Christ "always in my prayers" – follow me as I follow Christ

Verse 5

⁵ hearing of your love and faith which you have toward the Lord Jesus and toward all the saints, **Philemon 1:5**

In verse 4 it was Paul who exhibited saving faith. This is exactly what James meant by "faith without works (external evidence) is dead". True saving faith in the Living Christ always result in a changed life that cannot be hidden. Now watch how Philemon and the members of the church in his house.

1. "Hearing" – This means that they were living for Christ as it was evident to others. It reached Paul in Rome, over a thousand miles away.

2. "Love" – How do you know someone loves someone or something? It is revealed in the manner in which they treasure it. Let me ask you a question. What do you spend your time, thinking about, activities, listening to? That's what you treasure and love.

3. "Faith" – How do you evidence faith? By being bold to obey God irrespective of consequences. Will I stand for the Lord against the tide of family, friends, employment, coworkers, neighbors, government, the organized church, etc. Will I speak God's word if it means trouble and isolation? Will I be found faithful?

   [2] Moreover, it is required in stewards (slaves) **that one be found faithful. 1 Corinthians 4:2**

4. "Object of faith" – Beloved, our faith isn't in some speculation or some wishful thinking or a fad. Our faith is in a person who just so happens to be the Almighty God, Creator of heaven and earth. The believers' faith is in Christ, and it shows up in his love for fellow believers.

The scriptures tell us to have faith in God. This type of faith will persevere and cause the believer to act like the One in whom we believe, the Lord Jesus Christ. It is a life-altering faith. The surest evidence of saving faith is our love for the Lord shown in our unquenchable desire for His word, unwavering desire to obey His word, and love for our fellow believers in Christ. Fellow believers we have never seen or know of. When we hear about their persecution, we hurt along with them and instantly cry out to our God and Heavenly Father for deliverance, mercy, hope, joy, and peace. These are instantaneous and natural because of the bond formed in the Spirit of Christ with our Lord being the head of His body and we the body's members.

Basically, our faith in Jesus is evidenced in our love for the entire body of Christ from head to toe. This love is charitable, self-sacrificial, and performed in humility, not looking down on others or thinking more highly of ourselves than we should.

Verse 6

⁶ that the sharing of your faith may become effective by the acknowledgment of every good thing which is in you in Christ Jesus. **Philemon 1:6**

The early church did this most often. They shared everything.

³² Now the multitude of those who believed were of one heart and one soul; neither did anyone say that any of the things he possessed was his own, but they had all things in common. **Acts 4:32**

One must also remember that outside the nation of Israel, the world was controlled by Satan, with him as their god and king. Therefore, most people were slaves, not only to sin but to their earthly masters. What they worked for twelve hours each day only provided for their necessities that day, barely enough if they had children. They literally worked to feed themselves for one day. Those believers that had more, shared graciously with those who had little.

In this manner, a shared faith in the Lord Jesus Christ lived and walked in shoe leather, gave glory to God, and increased the effectiveness of the gospel. This is what the Apostle John meant when he spoke concerning this effective love of faith. (**1 John 3:16-23**)

This loving faith works is the outworking of love. In Philemon's case, this manifested itself in the realm of forgiveness.

Forgiveness? Yes. The forgiving of Onesimus, the slave who stole from his master and ran off to a foreign country to obtain some semblance of freedom. Will loving faith be evidenced through the gateway of forgiveness by Philemon in the power of the Holy Spirit? Or will he harbor bitterness, which will eventually evidence itself in its final forms of malice and wrath?

Are you saying that believers can behave in this manner? No, I didn't say that God did. Listen to the instructions the Apostle Paul gave to the church, believers, at Ephesus:

[30] And do not grieve the Holy Spirit of God, by whom you were sealed for the day of redemption. [31] Let all **bitterness, wrath, anger, clamor, and evil speaking be put away from you, with all malice. Ephesians 4:30-31**

The obvious answer to this question according to the scriptures is, of course believers can and do behave in this manner. Pain, sufferings, hurt feelings, false accusations, and disappointments are effective tools for the enemy to set his trap of bitterness, which leads to the final form of malice in wrath. This is the reason why the Holy Spirit speaks so often about controlling one's anger without sinning.

Now, realizing that there are some within Christianity who may hold to the assertion that true believers could never act in such a manner, but that is not a scriptural position. Why else would the Holy Spirit insert so many warnings in the scriptures to the church if it wasn't possible for them to commit such acts?

- Bitterness reflects a smoldering resentment.
- Wrath has to do with rage in the passion of a moment.
- Anger is an internal, deep hostility.
- Clamor is the outcry of out of control strife.
- Evil speaking is to slander someone's character.
- Malice is the desire to injure in various forms of evil ways.

What a scary scene! These are the behaviors that believers can conduct that lead to "grieving the Holy Spirit."

Then how do the believers combat these behaviors and prevent them from entering their hearts thereby impacting negatively, their relationship with others. From the heart, the believer must recognize the sin, repent immediately, then in the renewed power of the Spirit of God, obey the scriptures even if you do not like it or want to. Remember, we are slaves of Christ. Here our instructions are imperatives.

[32] And be kind to one another, tenderhearted, forgiving one another, even as God in Christ forgave you. **Ephesians 4:32**

The believer must purpose prior to the event that they will respond as instructed by the Holy Spirit.

- Be kind to one another. This speaks of a mild pleasant temperament.
- Tenderhearted is sympathetic compassion.
- Forgiving one another means to graciously restore as if the act never transpired and forget it ever happened by erasing the record of the wrongful action(s) from your mind.

Why? Because God has forgiven you, not based on your so-called good behavior. On the contrary, it is only because the penalty for your rebellion against a good and holy God was paid in full by Christ Jesus. Please do not get the idea that God forgives sinners on any other basis. Those, speaking of true believers, who have been forgiven so much by God should, of all people, forgive the relatively small offenses against them by others. We, today, still do not deserve God's forgiveness and never will. It is and will always only be by God's grace through faith in Christ. The most graphic illustration of this truth is the parable Jesus spoke in **Matt. 18:21–35.**

These things happen daily to believers and unbelievers. Jesus said it this way.

[24] "Therefore **whoever hears** these sayings of Mine, **and does them,** I will liken him to a wise man who built his house on the rock: [25] and the rain descended, the floods came, and the winds blew and beat on that house; and **it did not fall, for it was founded on the rock.** [26] "But **everyone who hears** these sayings of Mine, **and does not do them,** will be like a foolish man who built his house on the sand: [27] and the rain descended, the floods came, and the winds blew and beat on that house; **and it fell. And great was its fall."** **Matthew 7:24-27**

Who are the builders? They are true believers as the wise builder, and unbelievers as the foolish builder. What are the events that impact their homes? These are troubles, sorrows, disappointments, pain, sufferings, adversities, sickness, death, happiness, good times, and rejoicing. These are the ebbs and flow of life in a fallen world plagued and marred by sin. Jesus tells us that the true believers and unbelievers experience the same type of positive and negative events during their lifetime here on earth. The only difference is that one has a Savior, hence having a choice, and the other does not have a Savior and is a slave to his own sin. In Ephesians 4:31, we are commanded to "put these things away" from us because they do mental and physical harm to us and others but most distinctly it isn't pleasing to our Lord and grieves the Holy Spirit who resides within us.

Therefore, what is it that we ought to acknowledge? We are to acknowledge the deep, rich, full, experimental knowledge of the truth of God's word.

[15] Be diligent to present yourself approved to God, a worker who does not need to be ashamed, rightly dividing the word of truth. **2 Timothy 2:15**

The problem is that not all believers come to this knowledge of truth, which would enable them to rightly divine the word of God. Sadly, due to their lack of desire to commit time to the study of the word of God, most believers will never succumb to this knowledge of truth.

With respect to unbelievers, this knowledge is unobtainable.

[7] always learning and never able to come to the knowledge of the truth. **2 Timothy 3:7**

One must also be mindful that God's desires are not synonymous with God's purpose. They are not one and the same. For example, while God desires all people to be saved, we know according to scriptures that not all people will be saved. His desire led to providing a Savior, giving everyone the opportunity to be saved. His purpose for providing a Savior is to reconcile all things, meaning all creation, back to Himself eliminating the possibility that sin could ever enter His creation again. This paves the way for the entire Godhead to LIVE within the created WORLD.

All things made new.

¹ Now I saw a new heaven and a new earth, for the first heaven and the first earth had passed away. Also, there was no more sea. ² Then I, John, saw the holy city, New Jerusalem, coming down out of heaven from God, prepared as a bride adorned for her husband. ³ And I heard a loud voice from heaven saying, **"Behold, the tabernacle of God is with men, and He will dwell with them, and they shall be His people. God Himself will be with them and be their God**. ⁴ And God will wipe away every tear from their eyes; there shall be no more death, nor sorrow, nor crying. There shall be no more pain, for the former things have passed away." ⁵ Then He who sat on the throne said, "Behold, I make all things new." And He said to me, "Write, for these words are true and faithful." **Revelation 21:1-5**

The Glory of the New Jerusalem

²² But I saw no temple in it, for the Lord God Almighty and the Lamb are its temple. ²³ The city had no need of the sun or of the moon to shine in it, for the glory of God illuminated it. The Lamb is its light. ²⁴ And the nations of those who are saved shall walk in its light, and the kings of the earth bring their glory and honor into it. ²⁵ Its gates shall not be shut at all by day (there shall be no night there). ²⁶ And they shall bring the glory and the honor of the nations into it. ²⁷ **But there shall by no means enter it anything that defiles, or causes an abomination or a lie,** but only those who are written in the Lamb's Book of Life. **Revelation 21:22-27**

God's eternal purpose is to bring glory to His holy name.

¹² that we who first trusted in Christ should be to the praise of His glory. **Ephesians 1:12**

Is it possible for God to save everyone? Of course, it is. As a matter of fact, He can make it retroactive if that is what pleases Him. Yet, the scriptures declare that there will only be a remnant of people born on this planet that will enter life, heaven.

Why is that? It is to the praise of the glory of God's attributes through which His eternal purposes are being achieved. Listen to James as he addresses the early church counsel in Jerusalem.

³ And after they had become silent, James answered, saying, "Men and brethren, listen to me: ¹⁴ Simon has declared how God at the first **visited the Gentiles to take out of them** a people for His name. ¹⁵ And with this the words of the prophets agree, just as it is written:

¹⁶ 'After this I will return And will rebuild the tabernacle of David, which has fallen down; I will rebuild its ruins, And I will set it up; ¹⁷ So that the rest of mankind may seek the LORD, Even all the Gentiles who are called by My name, Says the LORD who does all these things.' ¹⁸ "Known to God from eternity are all His works." **Acts 15:13-18**

Does that sound like everyone will be saved to you? Now what about Israel? Listen to Paul as he tells us what the Holy Spirit says.

⁵ Even so then, at this present time **there is a remnant** according to the election of grace. ⁶ And if by grace, then it is no longer of works; otherwise, grace is no longer grace. But if it is of works, it is no longer grace; otherwise, work is no longer work. ⁷ What then? Israel has not obtained what it seeks; but **the elect have obtained it, and the rest were blinded. Romans 11:5-7**

I can hear it now from the skeptics, "Do you mean to say that God has blinded certain people?" No, I didn't say that; God did.

A careful reading of the whole of scriptures will present the entire picture, as the Lord did not say that He blinded anyone. Therefore, it is so important to read the entire Bible. Jesus said that He opened the eyes of the blind and gave light to those who sit in darkness.

[5] Thus says God the LORD, Who created the heavens and stretched them out, Who spread forth the earth and that which comes from it, Who gives breath to the people on it, And spirit to those who walk on it: [6] "I, the LORD, have called You in righteousness, And will hold Your hand; I will keep You and give You as a covenant to the people, As a light to the Gentiles, [7] To open blind eyes, To bring out prisoners from the prison, Those who sit in darkness from the prison house." **Isaiah 42:5-7**

[6] For it is the God who commanded light to shine out of darkness, who has shone in our hearts to give the light of the knowledge of the glory of God in the face of Jesus Christ. **2 Corinthians 4:6**

[17] I will deliver you from the Jewish people, as well as from the Gentiles, to whom I now send you, [18] to open their eyes, in order to turn them from darkness to light, and from the power of Satan to God, that they may receive forgiveness of sins and an inheritance among those who are sanctified by faith in Me.' **Acts 26:17-18**

[39] And Jesus said, "For judgment I have come into this world, that those who do not see may see, and that those who see may be made blind." [40] Then some of the Pharisees who were with Him heard these words, and said to Him, "Are we blind also?" [41] Jesus said to them, "If you were blind, you would have no sin; but now you say, 'We see.' Therefore, your sin remains. **John 9:39-41**

Does that sound like God is blinding people or giving the people who are already blind, sight? It's the latter. Every human is born into this world blind to the ways of God and dead to the presence of God. Only He can open our blinded eyes by His grace through faith in Jesus's death, burial, and resurrection.

This all stems from and has its origin in the Lord Jesus Christ. God for Christ's sake forgives every true believer. God does not and cannot forgive us by any other means or for any other reason. Since you and I are forgiven by grace through faith in Christ, we ought to be living examples of God's gracious forgiveness. However, we note that God has placed certain conditions on the offender and offended. The offender is to repent. The offended is to forgive. Jesus addressed this one day when Peter inquired about the number of times that we ought to forgive someone.

[21] Then Peter came to Him and said, "Lord, how often shall my brother sin against me, and I forgive him? Up to seven times?" [22] Jesus said to him, "I do not say to you, up to seven times, but up to seventy times seven." **Matthew 18:21-22**

What?! Seventy times seven? Yes, you read that correctly and that is daily.

Do you believe that that is some random arbitrary number selected by the Lord? Really? The Lord God does not do random. The phrase 70 x 7 = 490, which is the number of years to finish Israel's transgressions against Him. This is the seventy sabbaths of years that Israel refused to allow the land to rest as commanded in the Law of Moses. The references are 2 Chronicles 36:21, Leviticus 25:4-5, Jerimiah 25:8-12, Daniel 9, and Leviticus 26:34-35.

What are the good things in us that come after the acknowledgement of the truth? It is the fruit of the Spirit of God.

- Love
- Joy (not happiness, which depends upon circumstances)
- Peace
- Longsuffering
- Kindness
- Goodness
- Faithfulness
- Gentleness
- Self-control

We give up our rights to be right and to justify our ungodly behavior like anger, vengeance, and wrath. In return, we have imputed to us the peaceable fruit of righteousness by God's Spirit who resides in every true believer.

Oh beloved, how can it get any better than that! Yet it does. These things are in us through faith in Christ by God's grace empowered by the Holy Spirit to show the eternal glories of our Heavenly Father through the external works of loving faith that He had before ordained that we should walk in them. **Ephesians 2:10**

Most exciting is that all these things are taking place because of the true believer being positioned in Christ. Listen to our Lord.

[16] They are not of the world, just as I am not of the world. [17] Sanctify them by Your truth. Your word is truth. **John 17:16-17**

We died with Christ, [1] If (since) then you were raised with Christ, seek those things which are above, where Christ is, sitting at the right hand of God. ² Set your mind on things above, not on things on the earth. ³ For you died, and your (new) life (human spirit) is hidden with Christ in God. **Colossians 3:1-3**

This is how we ought to live because this is our reality. Look again at verses 1 and 2.

1. Seek, those things which are above – this is to earnestly crave, desire, and meditate upon
2. Set, your mind on things above – this is a fixation, a predetermined disposition

Did you notice the pattern? When we seek the heavenly things of Christ, the Lord promised that we will find them. What you will find is God's righteousness and His attributes.

³³ But seek first the kingdom of God and His righteousness, and all these things shall be added to you. **Matthew 6:33**

All these things, what things? God's righteousness and the knowledge of His attributes, which are His divine powers that gives us everything that pertains to life (the life of Christ for He is our life) and godliness (the earthly life modeled by Christ). This all comes "through the knowledge of Him who called us." How did You do that Lord? "By My own glory and virtue." Not our glory and virtue, for we have none nor will we ever have any of our own accord. This is how we become partakers of His divine nature. **2 Peter 1:2-4**

This is the reason Paul is commending Philemon. This is why Philemon should forgive.

Verse 7
⁷ For we have great joy and consolation in your love, because the hearts of the saints have been refreshed by you, brother. **Philemon 1:7**

In verse we learn the cause and effect of loving forgiveness. First the cause; "for we have great joy and consolation in your love."

Paul told us in verse 5 that Philemon's family and the Colossian church's love reached him in Rome. Their Christian lives were being lived out in their daily activities and walk with the Lord. Now, Paul communicates the results of this walking in the Spirit, the inescapable walk of love. This form of living brings joy. What then is joy? **Psalms 21:1** tells us that joy is only found in the Lord's strength and salvation. What then is God's strength? Three times in Exodus 13 we find this written: "by strength of hand the Lord brought us out". The Lord's strength is His ability to see, know, and guide His children at all times but especially during times of distress and anxiety. Exodus 15:2a says that the LORD is my strength and song and He has become my salvation. How then do we respond to God's gentle guidance and deliverance. Exodus 15:2b instructs us to declare, He is my God and I will praise Him; My father's God, and I will exalt Him. The proper response is to fall on our faces before Him with a heart of thanksgiving, worship, and praise. Now listen to Exodus 15:13, "You in Your mercy have led forth the people whom You have redeemed; You have guided them in Your strength to Your holy habitation." Oh beloved, how our God loves us. He will gently guide us with His eyes. Will you trust Him? Will you rest in Him? **Psalms 27:6** deals with a different issue, it addresses afflictions brought on by those who are the enemies of righteousness and truth. These enemies are not necessarily people as we are told in Ephesians 6, they are spirit beings using people to afflict God's children. These afflictions can easily cause a believer to fall into sin by becoming bitter, resentful, and hardened towards the person committing the offenses. The Psalmist tells us that God has already defeated these enemies therefore we should offer sacrifices of joy and sing praises to the LORD. Did you notice that joy is a sacrifice? We must endeavor to trust and believe the word of God thereby choosing to "sacrifice" our feelings on the alter of God's comfort which brings healing, rejoicing, peace, comfort, and joy. **Nehemiah 8:10** tells us of the broken hearts the children of Israel had during the years of captivity in Babylon and Persia when they heard the word of God for the first time when read by Nehemiah and Ezra.

Continuing our investigation of biblical joy, read the following references: **Isaiah 29:19; 35:10, Jeremiah 15:16, Habakkuk 3:18; Matthew 25:21; and 1 Thessalonians 1:6, 2:19.**

All these verses have one common theme. They all focus on the Lord and what He has accomplished, on behalf of God and the believer—what Jesus has done, is doing, and will do. That is joy beloved. Living with and for the Lord outside of our circumstances, not only do we have joy beyond our circumstances but comfort in them. This means that God is in absolute control of everything that is happening in our lives. **Isaiah 61:2; 2 Corinthians 1:3**

Acts 17:26 states, "God has determined our appointed times and the boundaries of our dwellings." You are not lost from the presence of God nor are you in a place where God has not placed you. You may be reaping what you have sown in accordance with the natural law of God governing this universe. However, His promise is to work all things for our God, for those who love God, to those who are the called, ACCORDING TO HIS OWN PURPOSE AND GOODNESS. **Romans 8:28**

There is no greater cry for God's comfort than the longing in the heart of the writer of Psalm 119. Listen to verse 50 when affliction is inflicted upon us by others.

[50] This is my comfort in my affliction, for Your word has given me life. **Psalms 119:50**

Verse 75 shows a different side of affliction. This affliction is actually chastisement or correction from the Lord Himself, that we may be partakers of His holiness. The Lord will never allow His children to live a sinful life.

[75] I know, O LORD, that Your judgments are right, and that in faithfulness You have afflicted me. **Psalms 119:75**

The Psalmist finds comfort in a life of affliction. "How?" you may ask.

Give me understanding, that I may learn Your commandments. **Psalms 119:73**

Because I have hoped in Your word. **Psalms 119:74**

For Your law is my delight. **Psalms 119:77**

But I will meditate on Your precepts. **Psalms 119:78**

Those who know Your testimonies. **Psalms 119:79**

Let my heart be blameless regarding Your statutes, **Psalms 119:80**

Comfort in the midst of affliction is found in the word of God. Oh, glory to God!

Joy is only found in the spirit realm beyond the circumstances of life. While comfort is only found in the physical realm amid the afflictions of a sin-filled, wicked, evil, and perverted humanity walking in the blindness of their flesh, hardness of their hearts, glorying in the uncleanness of their shame with greediness, whose father is the devil.

The Psalmist continues in **verse 76 of Psalm 119**; [76] Let, I pray, Your merciful kindness be for my comfort, according to Your word to Your servant.

Have you noticed a pattern between comfort in afflictions, difficult situations, knowing the word and ways of God? Listen to the Psalmist again in verses 81 & 82.

[81] My soul faints for Your salvation, but I hope in Your word. [82] My eyes fail from searching Your word, saying, "When will You comfort me?" **Psalms 119:81-82**

You can feel the Psalmist's pain. What did he do to relieve this pain? He relentlessly searched the word of God until he was totally exhausted physically and mentally. Why would he do that? Because he wanted to know what the word of God said about deliverance. His hope was in the truth of scriptures not in the present reality of his afflictions.

Finally, listen to Paul in **Romans 15:4-6**; [4] For whatever things were written before were written for our learning, **that we through the patience and comfort of the Scriptures might have hope.** [5] Now may the God of patience and comfort grant you to be like-minded toward one another, according to Christ Jesus, [6] that you may with one mind and one mouth glorify the God and Father of our Lord Jesus Christ.

WOW! Just wow! The word of God, learning about the attributes of God will teach us how God responds to our daily situations, is the key to comfort in afflictions and trying times. What does this have to do with forgiveness? Afflictions are the root cause of bitterness, which leads to an unforgiving heart.

Here are some final words of comfort from the Psalmist.

⁶⁷ Before I was afflicted, I went astray, but now I keep Your word. **Psalms 119:67**

⁷¹ It is good for me that I have been afflicted, that I may learn Your statutes. **Psalms 119:71**

¹⁰⁷ I am afflicted very much; revive me, O LORD, according to Your word. **Psalms 119:107**

That beloved is the cause of loving forgiveness. Now, let's examine the effect of loving forgiveness from the second half of verse 7.

1. The hearts of the saints – This is the bowels or inward affections of the believer. It is deeper than head knowledge. It's an outreach of tender mercies that a newborn baby feels from a loving parent.

2. Have been refreshed – This is a military word meaning to stand at rest. The command in the military is "at ease." To labor in order to recover and collect one's strength. This is the exact thing that happened to Peter. Our Lord told him that Satan desired to sift him as wheat, to afflict Peter that he would no longer be of use for the kingdom of God. Please understand that that is the sole purpose of the enemy's attacks. As believers, we are eternally secure in Christ having the record of our sins eradicated. Therefore, Satan cannot keep you out of heaven. However, he can limit or keep us from being an effective faithful witness of the gospel of Christ.

   Our Lord Jesus told Peter that He prayed for him that Peter's faith in God and faithfulness towards the work of God, should never fail in his afflictions at the hands of the devil. But Jesus did not stop there, He said to Peter, **when**

you recover and return to Me, strengthen your brothers. Luke 22:32

Have you read first and second Peter? Both letters are all about how to withstand afflictions and remain faithful in trials and tribulations. All believers will survive afflictions as well. Why? Because we are strong? We know the word of God? We are obedient slaves of Christ? We are faithful? Of course not! Although those things are characteristics of a mature believer and should be representative of our lifestyles, they in and of themselves are not the reason we survive afflictions and display a loving forgiving heart. The true reason is our Lord and Savior Christ Jesus prayed for us as well.

[20] "I do not pray for these alone, but also for those who will believe in Me through their word" **John 17:20**

THE WALK OF FORGIVENESS

Verse 8

[8] Therefore, though I might be very bold in Christ to command you what is fitting, **Philemon 1:8**

We now transition from the Character of Forgiveness to the Walk of Forgiveness. Note that verse 8 begins with "therefore." This is a clear reference to everything that was stated previously from verse 1 through 7. Since we now have a very good understanding of the character of God's forgiveness, we can now implement them in our daily walk with the Lord, a lifestyle of forgiveness.

Why would Paul make the statement "very bold in Christ"? Paul made this statement due to his apostolic authority given to the apostles of Christ. The scriptures clearly state that Christ and the apostles' doctrine are the foundation of the church. They were the men selected and assigned by the Lord Jesus to deliver His word to His elect, the true believers.

Why would Paul state that "he" could have "commanded" Philemon? Again, what Paul instructed Philemon to do was not from his own desire to lord over him. The commandment to receive Onesimus as a brother and forgive him came from the Lord, not Paul. Paul was the vessel to bring correction and instruction. However, this command was given by the Lord Jesus Himself in the gospels. Remember, 70 x 7. Let us look at a couple of other scripture references.

[31] Let all bitterness, wrath, anger, clamor, and evil speaking be put away from you, with all malice. [32] And be kind to one another, tenderhearted, **forgiving one another**, even as God in Christ forgave you. **Ephesians 4:31-32**

[12] Therefore, as the elect of God, holy and beloved, put on tender mercies, kindness, humility, meekness, longsuffering; [13] bearing with one another, and **forgiving one another, if anyone has a complaint against another; even as Christ forgave you, <u>SO YOU ALSO MUST DO.</u>** [14] But above all these things put on love, which is the bond of perfection. **Colossians 3:12-14**

Neither of these scriptures was written directly to Philemon, and the letter sent to him was written years after the epistle to the Ephesians and a few months after the epistle to the Colossians. Yet, they both have the same command from the Holy Spirit. We MUST forgive others because God, for Christ's sake, has forgiven us even though we don't deserve forgiveness and never will throughout all eternity. Nothing in these verses deals with our emotions, feelings, treatment, or any other human sentiments. The command is to forgive because you were forgiven, period, end of discussion. Paul put it this way, "what is fitting." It is the only behavior that receives approval from God; all others are considered sin.

Concerning masters who were slave owners and to the slaves, the Lord gives instructions on the relationship. Does He say to the masters, set them free? No, he does not. However, the true love for a brother compelled many to release their fellow brother or sister from bondage.

Slaves (Bondservants) and Masters

[5] Bondservants, be obedient to those who are your masters according to the flesh, with fear and trembling, in sincerity of heart, as to Christ; [6] not with eyeservice, as men-pleasers, but as bondservants of Christ, doing the will of God from the heart, [7] with goodwill doing service, as to the Lord, and not to men, [8] knowing that whatever good anyone does, he will receive the same from the Lord, whether he is a slave or free. [9] And you, masters, do the same things to them, giving up threatening, knowing that your own Master also is in heaven, and there is no partiality with Him. **Ephesians 6:5-9**

[1] Masters, give your bondservants what is just and fair, knowing that you also have a Master in heaven. **Colossians 4:1**

[1] Let as many bondservants as are under the yoke count their own masters worthy of all honor, so that the name of God and His doctrine may not be blasphemed. [2] And those who have believing masters, let them not despise them because they are brethren, but rather serve them because those who are benefited are believers and beloved. Teach and exhort these things. **1 Timothy 6:1-2**

[9] Exhort bondservants to be obedient to their own masters, to be well pleasing in all things, not answering back, [10] not pilfering, but showing all good fidelity, that they may adorn the doctrine of God our Savior in all things. **Titus 2:9-10**

[18] Servants, be submissive to your masters with all fear, not only to the good and gentle, but also to the harsh. [19] For this is commendable, if because of conscience toward God one endures grief, suffering wrongfully. [20] For what credit is it if, when you are beaten for your faults, you take it patiently? But when you do good

and suffer, if you take it patiently, this is commendable before God. [21] For to this you were called, because Christ also suffered for us, leaving us an example, that you should follow His steps: [22] "Who committed no sin, Nor was deceit found in His mouth"; [23] who, when He was reviled, did not revile in return; when He suffered, He did not threaten, but committed Himself to Him who judges righteously; [24] who Himself bore our sins in His own body on the tree, that we, having died to sins, might live for righteousness— by whose stripes you were healed. [25] For you were like sheep going astray, but have now returned to the Shepherd and Overseer of your souls. **1 Peter 2:18-25**

This is not an easy message to bring. Nevertheless, we have one Master, the Lord Jesus Christ, to whom we owe all. Nevertheless, O Lord God, your will be done!

Verse 9

9 Yet for love's sake I rather beseech thee, being such an one as Paul the aged, and now also a prisoner of Jesus Christ. **Philemon 1:9**

With this said, Paul preferred to yield towards love in lieu of commanding. He had a personal relationship with Philemon and cared deeply for him, knowing the character of Philemon. With this relationship and knowledge, would it be necessary to issue a command? No. Therefore, Paul used wisdom given by the Spirit of God to entreat his brother in Christ. Remember, what Paul told the Corinthians, that he could come in loaded for battle but would rather be loving, gentle, and kind.

Behold the subtle tact of Paul, "I'm an old man" and in prison for Christ, help a brother out.

Verse 10

10 I beseech thee for my son Onesimus, whom I have begotten in my bonds: **Philemon 1:10**

Why such pleading? Paul pleads with Philemon because it was customary during this period of time to put a runaway slave to death, especially a slave who had dishonored his master like Onesimus did by stealing from Philemon.

Paul tells Philemon, Onesimus is my son in the Lord. I personally led him to Christ while I was in prison. Although I am in prison, I am still doing the Lord's work and in the center of His will.

Is it proper to reason with someone when the word of God is clear on a specific command? Yes, of course it is, as some may not have the proper understanding of the whole counsel of the scriptures. The Lord Jesus gave us an example with the woman caught in adultery and the Samarian woman at the well. In the first reference, He reasoned with the people, then with the woman. In the second reference, He reasoned with the woman, then with the people. The results were the same. Both were forgiven and led to salvation, yet both, according to the law, should have been stoned to death. Yes, the Jews were still living under the law during the time Jesus was living on earth. The New Testament does not begin under after Christ died. In order for a testament which is another name for a will, to come into effect, the testator must be dead.

Like the Lord Jesus, in 1 Corinthians 5, Paul reasoned with the Corinthian church when they would not forgive the believer that was sleeping with his stepmother. You say, He did what? Slept with his stepmother? A true believer? Yes, that's what the scriptures state and no, God did not approve of that type of relationship, the scriptures clearly denunciates the behavior and calls it sin. Paul initially called for this believer to be expelled from the church and handed over to Satan for the destruction of the body (flesh), essentially the sin unto death spoken of in 1 John 5. But the man truly repented, and the church refused to forgive him and restore him to fellowship. Paul pleaded by stating that without the church, the man's sorrow would be too burdensome to bear. Therefore, for Christ's sake, restore him. ² Corinthians 2 There are many other examples of this posture in the scriptures, such as leaving the gift at the altar, to be reconciled to a brother, or addressing a fault one-on-one before going to get the elders, then elevating the matter to the entire church prior to expulsion.

Understand, beloved, that this is practical Christianity. This is walking the talk, living by faith, which works through love, following the Spirit, and obeying the word of God. Oh, sure, it is extremely difficult for us to perform when the pain and afflictions are fresh and the wounds are deep. The afflictions are multiplied when it involves a family member, both physical and spiritual. Just remember how the Lord forgives you and me daily for not being perfectly holy as He commands us to be, and sometimes, we willingly disobey.

Verse 11

Which in time past was to thee unprofitable, but now profitable to thee and to me: **Philemon 1:11**

Paul then states the obvious; Onesimus was unprofitable to you. I know what he did was wrong and will not attempt to belittle the offense. Paul did not attempt to hide or shy away from the truth of the facts. Onesimus was wrong and deserved the just punishment due according to Roman law which was death. Oh my, doesn't that sound like us before the Lord, the Holy One of Israel, dead in trespasses and sins deserving of eternal death? Guilty as charged and justly condemned, yes even now. Yet, the love, longsuffering, compassion, goodness, and forgiveness of our God through faith in the precious blood of Jesus Christ, His Son, has provided us acceptance and access to God's mercy and grace declaring us sons and daughters of the Most High God. Thank you, Lord! [1] Therefore being justified by faith, we have peace with God through our Lord Jesus Christ: 2 By whom also we have access by faith into this grace wherein we stand, and rejoice in hope of the glory of God. Romans 5:1-2

5 Having predestinated us unto the adoption of children by Jesus Christ to himself, according to the good pleasure of his will, 6 To the praise of the glory of his grace, wherein he hath made us accepted in the beloved. Ephesians 1:5-6

Paul now declares that something happened to Onesimus. He is now profitable, not only for you, Philemon, but to me as well. Christ has made Onesimus a new creature, and it is evident in his lifestyle. [17] Therefore if any man be in Christ, he is a new creature: old things are passed away; behold, all things are become new. 2 Corinthians 5:17 Onesimus' conversion is on display for all to read like an epistle. This is the external evidential work of saving faith that all true believers display openly to a dark, lost, dying, and ungodly world.

Has your faith changed you from being unprofitable for God to being profitable to the kingdom of Christ? If not, then your faith is not true saving faith. Saving faith is a life-altering metamorphosis, from death to life, from darkness to light, from unholy to holy, from ungodly to godliness. Onesimus began to walk in the light and walk in obedience to the word of God.

Verse 12

Whom I have sent again: thou therefore receive him, that is, mine own bowels: **Philemon 1:12**

Can you imagine the first conversation between Paul and Onesimus concerning returning to Philemon to be enslaved again? I can hear Onesimus' response now. What? You want me to do what? Are you kidding me? Paul, I don't want to be a slave again. Lovingly, Paul explains to Onesimus, "you never stop being a slave, Onesimus." Either you are a slave to sin and the devil or a slave to righteousness and Christ. Which are you? Repentance does not mean just saying I am sorry; it requires fruit worthy of true repentance. [7] Then said he to the multitude that came forth to be baptized of him, O generation of vipers, who hath warned you to flee from the wrath to come? 8 Bring forth therefore fruits worthy of repentance, and begin not to say within yourselves, We have Abraham to our father: for I say unto you, That God is able of these stones to raise up children unto Abraham. Luke 3:7-8 If you stole, you must pay it back fourfold. If you lied, you must come clean with the truth. This is true repentance in the eyes of God.

"I am sending Onesimus back to you because he is your slave." Wow, that does not seem fair. Of course, it is not fair. It is righteous and just, the true fruit of genuine repentance.

Have you repented of your sins to the Most High God? What then are the fruits of your repentance? The only fruit that you can give or offer is the fruit of obedience to the word of God from this day forward. You cannot repay God because it would take eternity and perfection; you and I don't possess either.

Remember Zacchaeus

¹ Then Jesus entered and passed through Jericho. ² Now behold, there was a man named Zacchaeus who was a chief tax collector, and he was rich. ³ And he sought to see who Jesus was, but could not because of the crowd, for he was of short stature. ⁴ So he ran ahead and climbed up into a sycamore tree to see Him, for He was going to pass that way. ⁵ And when Jesus came to the place, He looked up and saw him, and said to him, "Zacchaeus, make haste and come down, for today I must stay at your house." ⁶ So he made haste and came down, and received Him joyfully. ⁷ But when they saw it, they all complained, saying, "He has gone to be a guest with a man who is a sinner." ⁸ Then Zacchaeus stood and said to the Lord, "Look, Lord, I give half of my goods to the poor; and if I have taken anything from anyone by false accusation, I restore fourfold." ⁹ And Jesus said to him, "Today salvation has come to this house, because he also is a son of Abraham; ¹⁰ for the Son of Man has come to seek and to save that which was lost." **Luke 19:1-10**

Zacchaeus did not say, Lord, I have stopped stealing and then kept the money. No, no, no. He followed the law of restitution. Now, this fourfold restoration is part of the Mosaic Law and not in effect for the church. However, one must restore that in which we have offended.

To make this right with Philemon, Onesimus must return home and face the consequences of his actions. If you steal, Christian, you should go to jail. If you speed, you should be written a ticket. This is the law of sowing and reaping; Christians are not exempted from the natural and moral laws of God.

Paul's plea is for the life of Onesimus. Philemon, please do not put him to death. Would it be a sin for Philemon to put Onesimus to death? No, it would be just, nonetheless, Philemon has freedom in the Lord to forgive and restore. Is it wrong for a believer to desire the death penalty for someone who murders their loved one? No, it would be just, nonetheless, the believer has freedom in the Lord to forgive and restore.

In pleading, Paul states, don't put Onesimus to death. Do not cut off his hand. Paul, in the role of the Christ, asks Philemon in the role of God the Father, to please show Onesimus, in the role of the sinner, mercy **for my (Christ) sake.** " ... receive him, that is, my own heart (body)," Father. **Philemon 1:12b** [32] And be ye kind one to another, tenderhearted, forgiving one another, even as God for Christ's sake hath forgiven you. Ephesians 4:32

Verse 13

[13] whom I wished to keep with me, that on your behalf he might minister to me in my chains for the gospel. **Philemon 1:13**

Why, Paul, would you go to such extremes for Onesimus? Because Paul was in prison, and Onesimus was performing errands while learning the scriptures and being an encouragement to Paul. Paul had a companion who was faithful. He had already dispatched Timothy, Silas, and Titus to the care of the churches and needed another shoulder and soldier as Demas and others deserted him. The Lord sent Onesimus to Paul.

You may say, well, wait just one minute. Are you saying that God caused Onesimus to steal and run away so that he would be a minister to Paul? Of course not. That would be blasphemy. Onesimus' sinful actions were his own lustful desires, not the Lord's. [13] Let no man say when he is tempted, I am tempted of God: for God cannot be tempted with evil, neither tempteth he any man: 14 But every man is tempted, when he is drawn away of his own lust, and enticed. 15

Then when lust hath conceived, it bringeth forth sin: and sin, when it is finished, bringeth forth death. James 1:13-15 The Lord simply used the occasion to bring salvation to a lost soul. What if Onesimus did not run away? Would he have been saved? I will leave that for your consideration.

Paul takes liberty here with Philemon due to their friendship and states his desire, to keep Onesimus here with me in Rome so that the gospel may continue to reach people outside the prison walls. He is my brother at arms and a fellow soldier in the army of Christ. This Onesimus will do on your behalf? Yes, beloved. When we take part in the ministry of other believers, whether it be by prayer, financial support, time, or physical participation, these are accrued to the Lord's heavenly treasury in our account. This is gold, silver, and precious stones in the eyes of the Lord.

Verse 14
[14] But without your consent I wanted to do nothing, that your good deed might not be by compulsion, as it were, but voluntary. **Philemon 1:14**

Being fully aware that Onesimus was, in fact, the slave of Philemon, Paul was careful not to meddle in that affair. This is something that the word of God prohibits for believers.

[13] And besides they learn to be idle, wandering about from house to house, and not only idle but also gossips and busybodies, saying things which they ought not. **1 Timothy 5:13**

[9] But concerning brotherly love you have no need that I should write to you, for you yourselves are taught by God to love one another; [10] and indeed you do so toward all the brethren who are in all

Macedonia. But we urge you, brethren, that you increase more and more; [11] **that you also aspire to lead a quiet life, to mind your own business, and to work with your own hands, as we commanded you,** [12] that you may walk properly toward those who are outside, and that you may lack nothing. **1 Thessalonians 4:9-12**

[6] But we command you, brethren, in the name of our Lord Jesus Christ, that you withdraw from every brother who walks disorderly and not according to the tradition which he received from us. [7] For you yourselves know how you ought to follow us, for we were not disorderly among you; [8] nor did we eat anyone's bread free of charge, but worked with labor and toil night and day, that we might not be a burden to any of you, [9] **not because we do not have authority, but to make ourselves an example of how you should follow us.** [10] For even when we were with you, we commanded you this: If anyone will not work, neither shall he eat. [11] **For we hear that there are some who walk among you in a disorderly manner, not working at all, but are busybodies.** [12] Now those who are such we command and exhort through our Lord Jesus Christ that they work in quietness and eat their own bread. **2 Thessalonians 3:6-12**

If only we can get the body of Christ to stop being idle, gossiping, and busybodies, there would be much work accomplished for the kingdom of God. I will start with myself; will you join me?

Paul had the apostolic authority to command Philemon to allow Onesimus to remain with him in Rome. However, would that have been more beneficial for the cause of Christ, the furtherance of the gospel, the relationships of all involved, and the manner in which Philemon would have forgiven Onesimus? Absolutely not. Therefore, through the wisdom of the Holy Spirit, Paul deferred to love.

⁸ And above all things **have fervent love for one another**, for "love will cover a multitude of sins." **1 Peter 4:8**

The cover being spoken of is the blood of Jesus. God cannot simply love us into heaven. There must be a payment for our sins. Prior to being born into God's family, we were loveless, having no capacity to love God or anyone else. The scriptures declare that as the beloved of God we should love one another, for love is of God and everyone that loves is born of God and knows God. He that does not love, does not know God, **because God IS love**. God does not love as a behavior. No my friend. **God is love**. Dead people cannot love, dead in trespasses and sins.

¹² Therefore Jesus also, that He might sanctify the people with His own blood, suffered outside the gate. **Hebrews 13:12**

¹⁸ knowing that you were not redeemed with corruptible things, like silver or gold, from your aimless conduct received by tradition from your fathers, ¹⁹ but with the precious blood of Christ, as of a lamb without blemish and without spot. **1 Peter 1:18-19**

To truly forgive and experience true forgiveness, one must be born again in the spirit, by the Holy Spirit, and be in Christ, where the love of God is found. You heard that correctly. The love of God is found in a person, not in a place.

³⁸ For I am persuaded that neither death nor life, nor angels nor principalities nor powers, nor things present nor things to come, ³⁹ nor height nor depth, nor any other created thing, shall be able to separate us **from the love of God <u>which is in Christ Jesus our Lord</u>**. **Romans 8:38-39**

A voluntary act of release, allowing Onesimus to return to the ministry serving Paul, would be the ultimate picture of the Old Testament "scapegoat," a true picture of the sacrificial offering of the Lord Jesus by the Father, which granted freedom to the sinner to "escape" the righteous judgment and wrath of a holy God. Two goats were presented. Upon one fell the Lord's lot with that goat being offered up to God as a sin offering. But the goat on which the lot fell to be the scapegoat was presented "alive" (born again) before the Lord. The scapegoat was only alive because the atonement for the sinner's sin was paid by the first goat. After the blood of atonement was applied to the scapegoat, it was let go to escape back into the wilderness (the world) to be a witness to all concerning the atonement and freedom found in Christ.

Oh my, what a lovely type and picture of Christ. This is how the Lord expects us to lovingly forgive each other by remembering how and why He forgave us all our transgressions. This is so wonderful!

Verse 15

[15] For perhaps he departed for a while for this purpose, that you might receive him forever, **Philemon 1:15**

This is a marvelous verse. Have you ever considered where you are today in life: the nation in which you reside, the job which you now possess, the house in which you live. Has the thought entered your mind regarding past decisions that brought you to this place? Oh, the things we could have done differently. We could have been better children, better students, graduated from this school or that school, married this person, working in this profession, loving my career, had more or fewer children, been wealthier, healthier, and happier. Oh my, what I could have become, the places I could have visited, the things I could have accomplished. If only I would have done this, that, and the other thing, life would have been better.

Fair enough, but would you have been saved? Would you have heard the gospel, given the faith to believe by the Holy Spirit, repented of your sins, and believed upon Jesus Christ?

[26] For what profit is it to a man if he gains the whole world, and loses his own soul? Or what will a man give in exchange for his soul? **Matthew 16:26**

This is what Paul through the Holy Spirit was communicating to Philemon. Not that Paul was excusing or accusing God of being party to Onesimus' sins to bring him to Christ. May it never be. Our God is holy! May I put you in remembrance of what the scriptures declares.

[3] Let no one say when he is tempted, "I am tempted by God"; for God cannot be tempted by evil, **nor does He Himself tempt anyone.** [14] But **each one is tempted when he is drawn away by his own desires** and enticed. [15] Then, when desire has conceived, it gives birth to sin; and sin, when it is full-grown, brings forth death. **James 1:13-15**

It was Onesimus' desire to be free and to have a better life that caused him to sin. God had nothing to do with Onesimus' thefts, lies, deceits, and deception. God, however, did have a man, a slave, locked away in prison, perhaps for the sole purpose of preaching the gospel to Onesimus that he may be saved.

Onesimus was not looking for God or salvation. He thought by escaping Philemon's house, that he was free from being a slave, not understanding that he was still a slave to sin but now with a defiled conscience. Onesimus was seeking freedom, God sent a man chained to a Roman soldier day and night, in prison awaiting trial to tell Onesimus how to be free. No, not from Philemon, free from the wages of sin , free from being a slave of sin, free from being taken captive by the devil at his will. Although Onesimus was free from the man, Philemon, he was not free from the wrath of Almighty God.

[36] He who believes in the Son has everlasting life; and he who does not believe the Son shall not see life, **but the wrath of God abides on him." John 3:36**

[23] for all have sinned and fall short of the glory of God, **Romans 3:23**

[23] For the wages of sin is death, but the gift of God is eternal life in Christ Jesus our Lord. **Romans 6:23**

During one of the days when Onesimus went to work in the prison, he sat for a discussion with Paul. I'm certain Onesimus inquired of Paul; why Paul, are you in chains locked in this prison. The guard no doubt having listened to Paul preach daily could have spoken the answer. Paul's response shook Onesimus to his core, "I'm not the one wearing chains of bondage and locked in prison. You are!" Whoa! Wait! What?

Does Paul know about my past?, Onesimus must have wondered. How did he find out? Who could have told him? No one here in Rome knows me. Carefully, cautiously, and quietly, Onesimus whispered to keep the guard from overhearing his question. He asks, Do you know who I am, Mr. Paul?

Paul's answer brought Onesimus some temporary relief when he replied, No, I don't know who you are. That sweet relief soon turned into extreme fear when Paul further replied, But I know what you are. With a sincere confused look and a rapid heartbeat, Onesimus swallowed deeply and in a faint voice responded, What am I, Mr. Paul? Believing that his deep dark secret had come to light, Onesimus prepared to hear, you are a runaway slave from Colossea, and your master is searching for you.

Looking Onesimus directly in the eyes, Paul said, You are a sinner in need of a Savior, a child of the devil and a slave to your sins. Onesimus did a double take as he could not believe what he was hearing. He asked Paul, How can you say that about me when you do not know anything concerning my life? Paul's reply was genuine, loving, and caring, saying, I do not need to know you personally, Onesimus, to know what you are because I was once what you are, and so was everyone born of a man and a woman. What? stated a confused Onesimus. What are you talking about, Mr. Paul?

[16] Do you not know that to whom you present yourselves slaves to obey, you are that one's slaves whom you obey, whether of sin leading to death, or of obedience leading to righteousness? [17] But God be thanked that though you were slaves of sin, yet you obeyed from the heart that form of doctrine to which you were delivered. **Romans 6:16-17**

[20] For when you were slaves of sin, you were free in regard to righteousness. [21] What fruit did you have then in the things of which you are now ashamed? For the end of those things is death. **Romans 6:20-21**

Onesimus, my boy, says Paul as the chains rub the ground when he reaches out to touch his shoulder, you are indeed a slave to sin but do not worry or be fearful. I know the person who can set you free. Free, exclaimed Onesimus! Really, Mr. Paul, true freedom? Yes, Onesimus. The Lord Jesus whom I serve, for whom I am in these chains by whom I am here in this prison, can and will set you free if you believe in Him and repent of your sins.

[22] But now having been set free from sin, and having become slaves of God, you have your fruit to holiness, and the end, everlasting life. Romans 6:22

^{22} For he who is called in the Lord while a slave is the Lord's freedman. Likewise, he who is called while free is Christ's slave. **1 Corinthians 7:22**

How do you think Onesimus responded to the gospel?

^{31} Then Jesus said to those Jews who believed Him, "If you abide in My word, you are My disciples indeed. ^{32} And you shall know the truth, and the truth shall make you free." ^{33} They answered Him, "We are Abraham's descendants, and have never been in bondage to anyone. How can You say, 'You will be made free'?" ^{34} Jesus answered them, "Most assuredly, I say to you, whoever commits sin is a slave of sin. ^{35} And a slave does not abide in the house forever, but a son abides forever. ^{36} Therefore if the Son makes you free, you shall be free indeed." **John 8:31-36**

Onesimus departed from Philemon for the sole purpose of being free from the bondage of slavery. Philemon may have lost him for the remainder of each of their earthly lives. This is the case with every person born into this world. We are born separated from our Creator God, free from His loving presence all our earthly lives, slaves to sin.

Yet, God, who is a Savior who came to seek and to save that which is lost, found Onesimus in Rome, preached the gospel to him through Paul, gave Onesimus the faith to believe, and convicted him of his sins, causing Onesimus to repent and believe the gospel concerning the death, burial, and resurrection of Jesus Christ for the forgiveness of his sins. The Lord God requires blood to be shed as a payment for sin. That is the only acceptable payment to a holy, righteous, and just God. God cannot accept your good behavior, church attendance, baptism, repentance, penance, or any other benevolent acts. You may be asking, why not? The simply truth is none of those things contain blood which is the only acceptable payment.

[4] But God, who is rich in mercy, because of His great love with which He loved us, [5] even when we were dead in trespasses, made us alive together with Christ (by grace you have been saved), [6] and raised us up together, and made us sit together in the heavenly places in Christ Jesus, [7] that in the ages to come He might show the exceeding riches of His grace in His kindness toward us in Christ Jesus. [8] For by grace you have been saved through faith, and that not of yourselves; it is the gift of God, [9] not of works, lest anyone should boast. [10] For we are His workmanship, created in Christ Jesus for good works, which God prepared beforehand that we should walk in them. **Ephesians 2:4-10**

Are you seeking forgiveness? Are you seeking freedom from being a slave to sin? Cry out to Jesus to save you from your sin. There are no special words to say, but one must believe the record that God gave concerning the Jesus. That God laid upon Jesus all your sins and punished Jesus as if He had committed your sins in order to give you new life making you a child of God and providing freedom from the power of sin.

God's offer still stands today. Jesus is asking you today, [6] When Jesus saw him lying there, and knew that he already had been in that condition a long time, He said to him, "**Do you want to be made well?**" **John 5:6**

Well, do you?

Philemon lost a slave temporarily but gained a brother in Christ forever that not even physical death can take away. All glory, honor, and praise be to our God for His mercy endures forever and your truth Father, from generation to generation. Amen.

Verse 16

[16] no longer as a slave but more than a slave—a beloved brother, especially to me but how much more to you, both in the flesh and in the Lord. **Philemon 1:16**

Irrespective of Onesimus' spiritual position, as a child of God, he was still the property of Philemon. Even Paul noted that Onesimus would have never returned had Jesus, the only true Master, had not set him free from sin. Onesimus is no longer a slave to the lawlessness of the flesh, world, and the devil, no longer a captive to the lust of the eyes, the lust of the flesh, and the pride of life. (**1 John 2:15-17**) Onesimus has been regenerated, given a new heart–the operating system of life, translated out of the kingdom of Satan's darkness and into the kingdom of Christ's marvelous light. This is the evidence to God of salvation, not saying some sinner's prayer, attending church, reading the Bible, speaking gibberish, fake falling to the floor, any form of good righteous behavior. While those things may be good in the site of men, they cannot take away sin.

[17] Therefore, if anyone is in Christ, he is a new creation; old things have passed away; behold, all things have become new. 2 Corinthians 5:17

[15] For in Christ Jesus neither circumcision nor uncircumcision avails anything, but a new creation. Galatians 6:15

[25] Then **I will sprinkle** clean water on you, and you shall be clean; **I will cleanse** you from all your filthiness and from all your idols. [26] **I will** *give you a new heart and put a new spirit within you*; **I will** take the heart of stone out of your flesh and give you a heart of flesh. [27] **I will** put My Spirit within you and **cause you to walk** in My statutes, and **you will keep** My judgments and do them...you shall be My

people, and **I will** be your God. [29] **I will deliver** you from **all your uncleannesses. Ezekiel 36:25-29**

Only the blood of Christ can take away sin from the sinner. God is holy! He cannot forgive you any other way. There must be a payment for sin.

[22] And according to the law almost all things are purified with blood, and without shedding of blood there is no remission. **Hebrews 9:22**

[18] knowing that you were not redeemed with corruptible things, like silver or gold, from your aimless conduct received by tradition from your fathers, [19] but with the precious blood of Christ, as of a lamb without blemish and without spot. **1 Peter 1:18-19**

If Christ does not pay the debt to God for your sins, then you must pay the penalty for your sins. God said that penalty is to be cast into the lake of fire forever. That's how long it will take you to pay of your own sin debt.

The Great White Throne Judgment

[11] Then I saw a great white throne and Him who sat on it, from whose face the earth and the heaven fled away. And there was found no place for them. [12] And I saw the dead, small and great, standing before God, and books were opened. And another book was opened, which is the Book of Life. And the dead were judged according to their works, by the things which were written in the books. [13] The sea gave up the dead who were in it, and Death and Hades delivered up the dead who were in them. And they were judged, each one according to his works. [14] Then Death and Hades were cast into the lake of fire. This is the second death. [15] **And anyone not found written in the Book of Life was cast into the lake of fire. Revelation 20:11-15**

Are you really willing to take that chance?

Through the redemption and forgiveness of Christ, Onesimus is no longer just a slave to Philemon but a brother in Christ and an heir of the kingdom of God. How now, Philemon, are you to conduct yourself with a brother in Christ even though in the flesh he is your slave?

Paul reminds Philemon, Onesimus is more than just your slave to me. He is a fellow soldier in the army of the Most High God. Yet, even more so to you Onesimus is both a servant and a brother bringing twice the joy with forgiveness. Remember now, dear brother, how your Master treats you and do likewise. Work out of that soul salvation with reverence to His holy name. **(Phil. 2:12)**

Oh, the glory of being a slave to Christ!

Verse 17
[17] If then you count me as a partner, receive him as you would me.
Philemon 1:17

"If then," note that Paul is not questioning Philemon's affection towards him. Therefore, this use of the word "if" would be better understood as the "if" of argument and not that of condition. This would render the reading "Since you count me as a partner" in faith and service to Christ. They are on the same narrow road and straight path. They have one mind, the mind of Christ, to preach the everlasting gospel and reach as many people as possible. They have one Master whom to obey and follow.

Since all this is true, Philemon, treat Onesimus as you would treat me, not as an Apostle but as a brother and fellow laborer in Christ. Don't put him to death. Don't cut off his hand. Don't imprison him.

[12] Therefore, as the elect of God, holy and beloved, put on tender mercies, kindness, humility, meekness, longsuffering; [13] **bearing with one another, and forgiving one another**, if anyone has a complaint against another; even as Christ forgave you, **so you also must do** Colossians 3:12-13 Have someone injured you? Did they cause you pain that has scarred your memory so deeply that it comes to mind whenever you hear their name? Does it provoke you to anger and cause you to consider how to inflict the same upon them? The is real. The suffering is real. No amount of pretense can take it away. It happened, the scars are still visible the wounds are still open. Only the comfort of the scriptures, the hope of a life of eternal joy and peace through the healing grace of a loving heavenly Father can take such pain and anxiety away. Will you call upon Jesus today? Jesus is waiting to mend your broken heart by giving His life of peace and righteousness. Listen to what Jesus tells the Father.

Verse 18

[18] But if he has wronged you or owes anything, put that on my account. **Philemon 1:18**

Jesus tells the heavenly Father, if (insert your name) he/she sinned against you, owes you anything, place that burden upon Me. I will bare it on the cross. I willing offer up My life blood that (insert your name) may live, be healed and made well. Father forgive them for My name sake. Philemon, Paul continues, love Onesimus like you would me if I had wronged you.

Oh, please beloved listen to the gospel being preached in these verses. We owe God a debt for our sins. The penalty for sin is death. There must be a payment and restitution BEFORE there can be restoration and reconciliation. Paul is role playing Christ the redeemer in this verse. Onesimus is the sinner who rebelled and fled from God's presence like Adam with no way back nor was he interested in returning until Christ (Paul) came seeking and finding him.

Paul as Christ convinced Onesimus the sinner that he had the incorrect view of himself. Onesimus, you cannot justify your wicked behavior; you are wrong and need to change your opinion concerning what you are. You are guilty! You need to be reconciled back to Philemon who is role playing God the Father. However, before there can be reconciliation there must be a willingness from Onesimus the sinner, not only to admit his actions were wrong and worthy of just punishment due but a true willingness to return home to face judgment.

Do you really believe that when Paul first brought up that topic that Onesimus gleefully agreed to return home to be a slave again or even worst be put to death? I do not believe that was Onesimus' initial reaction for a second. I believe it took time before the Lord softened Onesimus's heart to bring him to the point of brokenness over his sin. This willingness to return home is a picture of true repentance. Repentance isn't just saying I am sorry for my actions. The scriptures states that there will always be the presence of righteous fruit or evidence when a sinner repents.

⁹ For they themselves (your righteous behavior) declare concerning us what manner of entry we had to you, and **how you turned to God from idols** to **serve the living and true God, 1 Thessalonians 1:9**

Listen to the Lord Jesus Christ preach the gospel at Paul's conversion.

¹⁷ I will deliver you from the Jewish people, as well as from the Gentiles, to whom I now send you, ¹⁸ **to open their (blinded) eyes, in order to turn them (sinners) from darkness to light,** and **(turn) from the power of Satan to God,** that they may receive forgiveness

of sins and an inheritance among those who are sanctified by faith in Me.' **Acts 26:17-18 – emphasis are mine.**

There was another problem standing in the way of reconciliation–restitution. How can an enslaved person who still has nothing, working twelve hours daily just to feed himself that day, restore that which he stole in accordance with Roman law? He owed far more than what he stole! Oh, what a helpless predicament Onesimus finds himself in!

Playing the role of Christ, Paul tells Philemon who plays the role of God the Father, "Put his sins on me." I will be the goat that is offered. Let Onesimus be the scapegoat.

⁴ Surely **He has borne** our griefs and carried our sorrows;
Yet we esteemed Him stricken,
Smitten by God, and afflicted.
⁵ But He was wounded for our transgressions,
He was bruised for our iniquities;
The chastisement for our peace was upon Him,
And by His stripes we are healed (**from what? The wrath of God upon our sins!**)
⁶ All we like sheep have gone astray;
We have turned, every one, to his own way;
And **the LORD has laid on Him the iniquity of us all**. Isaiah 53:4-6

¹⁰ Yet it pleased the LORD to bruise Him;
He has put Him to grief.
When You make His soul an offering for sin,
He shall see His seed, He shall prolong His days,
And the pleasure of the LORD shall prosper in His hand.
¹¹ He shall see the labor of His soul, and be satisfied.
By His knowledge My righteous Servant shall justify many,

For He shall bear their iniquities.
[12] Therefore I will divide Him a portion with the great,
And He shall divide the spoil with the strong,
Because He poured out His soul unto death,
And He was numbered with the transgressors,
And He bore the sin of many,
And made intercession for the transgressors. **Isaiah 53:10-12**

Has Jesus taken the wrath of God for your sins? If not my friend, you will have the wrath of God upon you forever. Cry out to Jesus for salvation right now by believing. Repent, begging God to forgive your sins for Christ's sake.

THE MOTIVE OF FORGIVENESS

Verse 19

[19] I, Paul, am writing with my own hand. I will repay—not to mention to you that you owe me even your own self besides. **Philemon 1:19**

Why would Paul tell Philemon that he wrote this letter "with my own hand?" Most likely because most of the letters to the churches were dictated by Paul but recorded by a scribe and he would sign the letter. This time, Paul did not dictate, nor did anyone assist the writing nor the content.

Likewise, Christ, by His own volition and predetermined will, took upon Himself the wrath of God in payment for our sins to secure our forgiveness from the Father forever.

[17] "Therefore My Father loves Me, **because I lay down My life that I may take it again.** [18] **No one takes it from Me, but I lay it down of Myself.** I have power to lay it down, and I have power to take it again. This command I have received from My Father." **John 10:17-18**

[3] who being the brightness of His glory and the express image of His person, and upholding all things by the word of His power, **when He had by Himself purged our sins**, sat down at the right hand of the Majesty on high, **Hebrews 1:3**

[10] By that will we have been sanctified through the offering of the body of Jesus Christ once for all ... [12] But this Man, after He had offered one sacrifice for sins forever, sat down at the right hand of God, [13] from that time waiting till His enemies are made His footstool. [14] For by one offering He has perfected forever those who are being sanctified. **Hebrews 10:10, 12-14**

Remember the word of God is only about three things.

- The revelation of the one true God
- The reconciliation plan of God
- The restoration of creation by God

It is not about you and me receiving something from God. This letter continues in that theme by revealing the gospel to us through the role play of the characters. Philemon as God the Father, Paul as Christ, and Onesimus as the sinner in need of forgiveness he does not and will never deserve.

The theme of the Old Testament is the God the Savior concealed. The theme of the New Testament is the God the Savior revealed. The theme of Revelation is the God the Savior enthroned.

Jesus, like Paul, says Father (Philemon), put it on my account. Whatever Onesimus the sinner owes You, I will repay in full. How did the Father respond?

[10] Yet **it pleased the LORD to bruise Him**; He has put Him to grief.

When You make His soul an offering for sin, He shall see His seed, He shall prolong His days, and the pleasure of the LORD shall prosper in His hand. [11] He shall see the labor of His soul, and be satisfied. By His knowledge My righteous Servant shall justify many, For He shall bear their iniquities. [12] Therefore I will divide Him a portion with the great, And He shall divide the spoil with the strong, because He poured out His soul unto death, and He was numbered with the transgressors, And He bore the sin of many, and made intercession for the transgressors. **Isaiah 53:10-12**

Why would it please the Father to bruise His own Son? So that the Holy One of Israel would not have to bruise you and me but offer us forgiveness and the impute to us the righteousness of Christ. What does this have to do with Paul and Philemon? Philemon had the choice of forcing Onesimus to pay the penalty for his crimes but instead Paul requested that Philemon subject him to the punishment and he would pay restitution, thereby allowing Philemon to fully impute forgiveness onto Onesimus. What role did Onesimus play? As the sinner, he simply received the forgiveness and repented for the wrongs he committed. Then lived the remainder of his life in service to his masters who paid the price and forgave him freely. Masters? Yes, remember this is role play; the Father and Jesus are One God.

Now, this is a very interesting comment made by Paul. "…not to mention to you that you owe me even your own self besides." What in the world is Paul talking about?

Well, it was Paul who preached the gospel to Philemon when he was pastoring the church at Ephesus. Philemon was living in Ephesus at that time and was led to the Lord by Paul. Therefore, Paul is also Philemon's spiritual father. So, what does Philemon owe Paul? His life. No, not his physical birth, his spiritual regeneration through the belief of the gospel preached. No gospel preached then no belief, then of course no salvation by grace through faith in Jesus.

Then what is the connection of this declaration as it relates to Christ and the Father? How can Christ say to the Father, "you owe me even your own self besides?"

[17] "Therefore My Father loves Me, **because I lay down My life** that I may take it again." **John 10:17**

Because the Son lays down His life the Father gives Christ certain promises.

The first promise to Jesus was made by God prior to creation when the Godhead called forth the Man to be presented to themselves.

[8] But to the Son He says: "Your throne, O God, is forever and ever; A scepter of righteousness is the scepter of Your kingdom. [9] **You have loved righteousness and hated lawlessness; Therefore God, Your God, has anointed You** with the oil of gladness more than Your companions." **Hebrews 1:8-9**

The second promise to Jesus was made by God after the resurrection.

[6] "Yet I have set My King on My holy hill of Zion." [7] "I will declare the decree: The LORD has said to Me, You are My Son, today I have begotten You. [8] **Ask of Me, and I will give You the nations for Your inheritance, and the ends of the earth for Your possession.**" **Psalms 2:6-8**

The Son, the Lord Jesus Christ, after fulfilling all the prophesies and receiving all the promises made by the Father, then gives everything back into the Father's hands for Him to distribute as He pleases and be Lord over all and in all.

[20] But now Christ is risen from the dead, and has become the firstfruits of those who have fallen asleep. [21] For since by man came death, by

Man also came the resurrection of the dead. [22] For as in Adam all die, even so in Christ all shall be made alive. [23] But each one in his own order: Christ the firstfruits, afterward those who are Christ's at His coming. [24] Then comes the end, when He delivers the kingdom to God the Father, when He puts an end to all rule and all authority and power. [25] For He must reign till He has put all enemies under His feet. [26] The last enemy that will be destroyed is death. [27] For "He has put all things under His feet." But when He says "all things are put under Him," it is evident that He who put all things under Him is excepted. [28] Now when all things are made subject to Him, then the Son Himself will also be subject to Him who put all things under Him, that God may be all in all. **1 Corinthians 15:20-28**

It was always the Father's plan to enter the created world to live, tabernacle, among His creation but there was a serious problem that needed to be resolved prior to the Godhead taking up permanent residency in the created world. The possibility of sin!

Oh, beloved, please understand that the entirety of the scriptures is about the Father ridding His creation from even the possibility of sin ever happening again. Then living among His creation forever.

Read the scriptures below slowly and carefully.

[1] Now I saw a new heaven and a new earth, for the first heaven and the first earth had passed away. Also, there was no more sea. [2] Then I, John, saw the holy city, New Jerusalem, coming down out of heaven from God, prepared as a bride (prepared as (or like) a bride, it is not the bride) adorned for her husband. [3] And I heard a loud voice from heaven saying, **"Behold, the tabernacle of God is with men, and He will dwell with them, and they shall be His people. God Himself will be with them and be their God.** [4] And God will wipe away every tear

from their eyes; there shall be no more death, nor sorrow, nor crying. There shall be no more pain, for the former things have passed away." [5] Then He who sat on the throne said, "Behold, I make all things new." And He said to me, "Write, for these words are true and faithful." [6] And He said to me, "**It is done! (God has eliminated the possibility of sin from ever entering His creation again, now the Father can enter the world fully)** I am the Alpha and the Omega, the Beginning and the End. I will give of the fountain of the water of life freely to him who thirsts. [7] He who overcomes shall inherit all things, and I will be his God and he shall be My son. [8] **But the cowardly, unbelieving, abominable, murderers, sexually immoral, sorcerers, idolaters, and all liars shall have their part in the lake which burns with fire and brimstone, which is the second death." Revelation 21:1-8**

Here is the second half of the prophecy.

[22] But I saw no temple in it, **for the Lord God Almighty and the Lamb are its temple.** [23] The city had **no need of the sun or of the moon** to shine in it, for the **glory of God illuminated it** (notice the drastic change of the environment). **The Lamb is its light.** [24] And the nations of those who are saved shall walk in its light, and the kings of the earth bring their glory and honor into it. [25] Its gates shall not be shut at all by day (**there shall be no night there**). [26] And they shall bring the glory and the honor of the nations into it. [27] **But there shall by no means enter it anything that defiles, or causes an abomination or a lie**, but only those who are written in the Lamb's Book of Life. **Revelation 21:22-27**

I want to focus on this statement because this is the meat of what the Lord has accomplished and what is being played out in our lives and the future until this ultimately is fulfilled.

<u>²⁷ But there shall by no means enter it anything that defiles, or causes an abomination or a lie</u>

Let's break this down into segments. What is the topic? Heaven. Where is heaven? Heaven is wherever God is. No, it is not some destiny in outer space. It is literally according to the scriptures outside of the created world where the Godhead alone reside.

You are probably asking yourself, from where did he arrive at that conclusion? I will not get into hermeneutics principles of biblical interpretation which basically means, to read the scriptures. However, I will show you how the scriptures conclude that the Godhead exists outside of creation.

First, we start with the holiness of God.

¹³ **You (God) are of purer eyes than to behold evil and cannot look on wickedness.** Why do You look on those who deal treacherously, and hold Your tongue when the wicked devours a person more righteous than he? **Habakkuk 1:13**

Beloved, the God of all creation cannot look upon sin, any sin, without annihilating it. What do I mean by sin? This means that if any created thing does not remain in the exact way that God created it, it is sin in His eyes. This is what Paul was talking about in Romans when he recorded these words.

²³ for all have sinned and **fall short of the glory of God, Romans 3:23**

We all fall short of God's glory because none of us are like God created the first man, Adam, prior to the fall. Just our mere birth is sin in the eyes of a holy God. Okay, let us continue. Notice next that God sent His Son "into the world." What does that mean? If I am standing at the front door of your home knocking, then you open the door and say to me, come "into my home." Was I already inside your home? Of course not. One can only come into something if you are outside of it. Does world mean the earth only? Not according to the scriptures. Please pay close attention to the progression in the book of Hebrews.

[6] But when He again brings the firstborn **into the world**, He says: "Let all the angels of God worship Him." **Hebrews 1:6**

If "world" means earth then all the angels, holy and unholy reside here on earth. Obviously, that is incorrect theology. Therefore, "world" cannot mean planet earth.

Paul declared that the apostles were spectacles to the "world."

[9] For I think that God has displayed us, the apostles, last, as men condemned to death; for we have been made a **spectacle to the world**, both to angels and to men. **1 Corinthians 4:9**

Paul included angels and men just like the writer of Hebrews as both being in the "world."

[5] Therefore, when He (Jesus the Firstborn) came **into the world**, He said: "Sacrifice and offering You (the Godhead) did not desire, but a body You have prepared for Me." Hebrews 10:5

When was this body created? According to the scriptures, Jesus's body was sacrificed before the creation of the world.

[8] All who dwell on the earth will worship him, whose names have not been written in the Book of Life of the **Lamb slain from the foundation of the world. Revelation 13:8**

The scriptures declares that God was in Christ reconciling the world to Himself, things on earth or in heaven. Wait, what? If heaven is holy and God is there, why would He have to reconcile anything in heaven? That's because the heavens of this world are not holy; they are atoned by the blood of the cross.

¹⁹ For it pleased the Father that in Him all the fullness should dwell, ²⁰ and **by Him to reconcile all things to Himself, by Him, whether things on earth or things in heaven**, having made peace through the blood of His cross. **Colossians 1:19-20**

This verse basically states that the real heaven where God alone resides is at peace with the heavens of this world because of the blood of Christ. This blood was shed before the heavens and earth were created, which allowed God to create them both and their inhabitants.

¹⁷ For God did not send His Son **into the world** to condemn the world, but **that the world through Him might be saved. John 3:17**

Will the world be saved? Not according to scriptures. The scriptures declare that this present "world," which includes both the heavens and the earth, will be totally annihilated in a cosmic meltdown. By the way, the earth includes the entire physical universe not just the planet. If man can discover it, see it, or touch it, it is part of "earth." Now listen to the scriptures.

³¹ **Heaven and earth will pass away**, but My words will by no means pass away. **Mark 13:31**

As part of the finality of the "Day of the Lord," which includes the physical bodily return of our Lord and Savior Jesus Christ, the 1,000-year Millennium reign of Christ, the Great White Throne Judgment, the casting of the devil, the demonic hosts, and all unbelievers into the lake of fire, this will happen.

[10] But the day of the Lord will come as a thief in the night, **in which the heavens will pass away with a great noise, and the elements will melt with fervent heat; both the earth and the works that are in it will be burned up.** [11] Therefore, since **all these things will be dissolved**, what manner of persons ought you to be in holy conduct and godliness, [12] looking for and hastening the coming of the day of God, **because of which the heavens will be dissolved, being on fire, and the elements will melt with fervent heat?** [13] Nevertheless we, according to His promise, **look for new heavens and a new earth in which righteousness dwells. 2 Peter 3:10-13**

When these new heavens and a new earth are created by the Lord Jesus Christ, then and only then will the Godhead enter into the newly created world. Listen to the scriptures.

[20] But now Christ is risen from the dead, and has become the firstfruits of those who have fallen asleep. [21] For since by man came death, by Man also came the resurrection of the dead. [22] For as in Adam all die, even so in Christ all shall be made alive. [23] But each one in his own order: Christ the firstfruits, afterward those who are Christ's at His coming. [24] Then comes the end, when He delivers the kingdom to God the Father, when He puts an end to all rule and all authority and power. [25] For He must reign till He has put all enemies under His feet. [26] The last enemy that will be destroyed is death. [27] For "He has put all things under His feet." But when He says "all things are put under Him," **it is evident that He who put all things under Him is excepted.** [28] **Now when all things are made subject to Him, then the Son Himself will also be subject to Him who put all things under Him, that God may be all in all. 1 Corinthians 15:20-28**

Watch what happens after the current world, which includes the heavens and the earth, is destroyed.

[1] **Now I saw a new heaven and a new earth, for the first heaven and the first earth had passed away**. Also, (notice the change in topography) <u>there was no more sea</u>. [2] Then I, John, saw the holy city, New Jerusalem, coming down out of heaven from God, prepared as a bride adorned for her husband. [3] And I heard a loud voice from heaven saying, **"Behold, the tabernacle of God is with men, and He will dwell with them**, and they shall be His people. God Himself will be with them and be their God. [4] And God will wipe away every tear from their eyes; there shall be no more death, nor sorrow, nor crying. There shall be no more pain, **for the former things (the old world consisting of the old heavens and earth) have passed away." Revelation 21:1-4**

Heaven will have no sun or moon. They are no longer necessary.

[22] But I saw no temple in it, for the Lord God Almighty and the Lamb are its temple. [23] The city had **no need of the sun or of the moon to shine in it, for the glory of God illuminated it.** The Lamb is its light. [24] And the nations of those who are saved shall walk in its light, and the kings of the earth bring their glory and honor into it. [25] Its gates shall not be shut at all by day (**there shall be no night there**). [26] And they shall bring the glory and the honor of the nations into it.

Now, read this very carefully. There will never ever be sin in God's creation ever again. This is the only reason why the Most High and Holy God can come into the created world. Only those who love God will be residents of the new heavens and earth, both angels and humans. Therefore, all will remain in the state in which God created them.

²⁷ But there **shall by no means enter it anything that defiles, or causes an abomination or a lie**, but only those who are written in the Lamb's Book of Life. **Revelation 21:22-27**

Therefore, Paul as Christ communicates to Philemon as the Father, "no worries, Father, I will never mention to You that which I willingly do, laying down My life for Your glory. For My will is to glorify You not Myself. That You be glorified is My eternal reward."

Verse 20

²⁰ Yes, brother, let me have joy from you in the Lord; refresh my heart in the Lord. **Philemon 1:20**

Jesus prayed this to the Father. I only ask this of You. I desire that they also whom You gave Me may be with Me where I am, that they may behold (witness) My glory which You have given Me. Paul requested the same of Philemon, that Onesimus be with him to glorify the Lord.

By the way, what was the glory of Jesus? He said it was to do the will and work of Him who sent Me.

Jesus continued in prayer. For You, Father, loved Me (this is the only true motive for our Lord forgiving us and should be our motive to forgive others) before the foundation of the world. This is from the prayer our Lord prayed in John 17.

What was Paul's joy?

¹⁹ For what is our hope, or joy, or crown of rejoicing? **Is it not even you in the presence of our Lord Jesus Christ at His coming? 1 Thessalonians 2:19**

Paul's joy was the salvation of others. The primary purpose of the true believer's life while living on this earth is to obey the Lord by preaching the gospel to the lost thereby bringing others to heaven with you. All this other foolishness about health, wealth, and happiness is garbage and blasphemy to the cause of Christ.

Philemon, forgive Onesimus for my sake. I love him.

Father, forgive Kevin for My (Jesus) sake. I love him.

Father, forgive me (you) for Jesus's sake. He loves me and died for me.

I love them! I will pay the restitution. I will reconcile them to You. Let them stay with Me, for Your mercy and grace sake, that they may behold My glory which You gave Me before the world was created.

Wow, the gospel preached in Philemon!

Verse 21
²¹ Having confidence in your obedience, I write to you, knowing that you will do even more than I say. **Philemon 1:21**

Our Lord and Savior Jesus Christ willingly obeyed the Father by humbling Himself. He took upon Himself the body of a man, a slave to the Father, to free those who were slaves to sin.

¹⁹ For as by one man's (Adam) disobedience many were made sinners, so also by one Man's (Jesus) obedience many will be made righteous. **Romans 5:19**

Please note that the "many" in this verse is the same group of people. These are the humans whose names were "…written in the Book of Life from the foundation of the world…." Revelation 17:8

⁴ just as **He chose us in Him before the foundation of the world**, that we should be holy and without blame before Him in love,

⁵ having predestined us to adoption as sons by Jesus Christ to Himself, according to the good pleasure of His will, ⁶ to the praise of the glory of His grace, by which He made us accepted in the Beloved. **Ephesians 1:4-6**

You, Lord Jesus, did more than any other could ever do, for I (Onesimus) offended You Master (the Father). Therefore, I beg for your forgiveness.

²⁵ Therefore He (Jesus) is also able to save to the uttermost those who come to God through Him, since He always lives to make intercession for them. **Hebrews 7:25**

Our hearts and minds cannot fully comprehend what You, Lord Jesus, have accomplished on our behalf.

¹ Behold what manner of love the Father has bestowed on us, that we should be called children of God! Therefore the world does not know us, because it did not know Him. ² **Beloved, now we are children of God; and it has not yet been revealed what we shall be, but we know that when He is revealed, we shall be like Him, for we shall see Him as He is.** ³ And everyone who has this hope in Him purifies himself, just as He is pure. **1 John 3:1-3**

Verse 22

²² But, meanwhile, also prepare a guest room for me, for I trust that through your prayers I shall be granted to you. **Philemon 1:22**

This is so wonderful. Paul is requesting that a room be prepared in the Philemon's house. What does this remind you of?

¹ "Let not your heart be troubled; you believe in God, believe also in Me. ² In My Father's house are many mansions; if it were not so, I

would have told you. I go to prepare a place for you. ³ And if I go and prepare a place for you, I will come again and receive you to Myself; that where I am, there you may be also. ⁴ And where I go you know, and the way you know." **John 14:1-4**

Our resurrected Lord has gone to the Father's house to prepare a place for us. He is preparing a room for us in the New Jerusalem, which is the temple of God. The scriptures describe what the New Jerusalem looks like in Revelation 21. You can read that entire chapter for the details. In Revelation 22, the scriptures provide a brief description of the inside of the New Jerusalem and mentions its residents.

¹ And he showed me a pure river of water of life, clear as crystal, proceeding from the throne of God and of the Lamb. ² In the middle of its street, and on either side of the river, was the tree of life, which bore twelve fruits, each tree yielding its fruit every month. The leaves of the tree were for the healing of the nations. ³ **And there shall be no more curse, but the throne of God and of the Lamb shall be in it, and <u>His servants shall serve Him</u>.** ⁴ They shall see His face, and His name shall be on their foreheads. ⁵ There shall be no night there: They need no lamp nor light of the sun, for the Lord God gives them light. **And they shall reign forever and ever. Revelation 22:1-5**

This is the "room" that is being prepared for every true believer. The servants, which is really the word slaves, that are serving Him are the true believers. That's us. The scriptures declares that we will reign with Christ forever and ever as His forgiven slaves. What right then do we have to not forgive one another?

Note that Paul states that it is through prayers that deliverance is granted. It is Christ and the Holy Spirit who constantly pray for us before the Father, just as we are instructed by the Lord to pray for the body of Christ.

[25] Therefore He is also able to save to the uttermost those who come to God through Him, **since He always lives to make intercession for them. Hebrews 7:25**

[26] Likewise the Spirit also helps in our weaknesses. For we do not know what we should pray for as we ought, **but the Spirit Himself makes intercession for us** with groanings which cannot be uttered. [27] Now He who searches the hearts knows what the mind of the Spirit is, **because He makes intercession for the saints according to the will of God. Romans 8:26-27**

[34] Who is he who condemns? It is Christ who died, and furthermore is also risen, who is even at the right hand of God, **who also makes intercession for us. Romans 8:34**

[17] pray without ceasing, **1 Thessalonians 5:17**

Now listen to the Lord Jesus in His request to the Father specifically for the true believers.

[9] "I pray for them. I do not pray for the world but for those whom You have given Me, for they are Yours..." [20] "I do not pray for these alone, but also for those who will believe in Me through their word" **John 17:20; John 17:9**

Finally, the Lord Jesus caps off the prayer with this request.

[24] **"Father, I desire that they also whom You gave <u>Me may be with Me where I am,</u>** that they may behold My glory which You have given Me; for You loved Me before the foundation of the world." **John 17:24**

The Lord is praying that we join Him with the Father in the New Jerusalem. Revelation reveals that God has already answered this prayer. We are only waiting for the fullness of time for this to become our reality. What a wonderful future God has in store for those who believe in His Son.

Can you hear the discussion between the Son and the Father?

In the meantime, Father, until My return to the earth, allow Me to prepare a place for them, a room in Your house. They can trust Me to do exactly what I promised. I will come again and receive you to Myself that where I am, you will be also.

Paul fully expected Philemon to receive both he and Onesimus. Because Paul (in the role of Jesus) knows Philemon (in the role of the Father) has accepted Onesimus (us, the sinner) in the beloved (the beloved Son). **Ephesians 1:6; Romans 5:1-11**

What a precious promise! What glory awaits us knowing that every promise in Christ is yes and amen!

Verse 23
[23] Epaphras, my fellow prisoner in Christ Jesus, greets you, **Philemon 1:23**

Epaphras, who was the pastor and founder of the church at Colossea, was also in Rome seeking guidance from Paul when this letter was penned. Epaphras also came to faith in Christ through Paul's ministry when Paul was teaching in Ephesus. He received the letter to the Colossian church, which deals with the heresy called gnosticism. Gnosticism is the belief that God is good, but matter is evil, that Jesus Christ was merely one of a series of emanations descending from God and being less than God. This is basically a belief that led them to eventually deny Christ' true humanity. It also led some in the church, these false believers, to claim that some secret, higher knowledge above scripture was necessary for enlightenment and salvation. Today, part of this false doctrine is called monolicism. The higher knowledge has found roots in the church through the requirements of speaking in tongues, visions, out of body experiences, water baptism, prayer languages, being filled with the Holy Spirt, etc. which leads some to be puffed up by external experiences instead of the word of God. Though they claim to have these experiences almost daily, their knowledge of the word of God is deficient because they prefer to seek experiences in lieu of sitting at the feet of our Master and eating His words.

The Colossian gnosticism heresy also embraced aspects of Jewish legalism, which essentially was the requirement of circumcision for salvation, observance of the ceremonial rituals of the OT law (dietary laws, festivals, Sabbaths), and rigid asceticism. Asceticism is the requirement of strict dietary restrictions like the vow of a Nazarene.

It also called for the worship of angels and mystical experience. Epaphras was so concerned about this heresy that he journeyed over one thousand miles from Colossea to Rome, where Paul was a prisoner. You can read the book of Colossians to view the Lord's response to these heresies.

Epaphras knew Philemon well as he was Philemon's pastor. Apparently, Epaphras did not return to Colossea at the time this letter was sent to Philemon.

Verse 24
[24] as do Mark, Aristarchus, Demas, Luke, my fellow laborers. **Philemon 1:24**

Note the men who were ministering with Paul during his imprisonment in Rome. Mark and Aristarchus were the two faithful Jews. Of course, Mark was an example to Philemon because of his past experience with Paul. Remember, it was a disagreement concerning Mark that he and Barnabas separated. Mark had deserted them during their second missionary journey. Therefore, Paul was refusing to take him on the third missionary journey. Yet, Mark was Barnabas's cousin. Therefore, he did not want to give up on him.

[36] Then after some days Paul said to Barnabas, "Let us now go back and visit our brethren in every city where we have preached the word of the Lord, and see how they are doing." [37] Now Barnabas was determined to take with them John called Mark. [38] But Paul insisted that they should not take with them the one who had departed from them in Pamphylia, and had not gone with them to the work. [39] Then the contention became so sharp that they parted from one another. And so Barnabas took Mark and sailed to Cyprus; [40] but Paul chose Silas and departed, being commended by the brethren to the grace of God. [41] And he went through Syria and Cilicia, strengthening the churches. **Acts 15:36-41**

Paul later forgave Mark, and their relationship was restored, with Paul later stating that Mark is profitable to me for the ministry. Mark eventually was discipled by Peter, writing the gospel of Mark, as Peter narrated the events.

[11] Only Luke is with me. Get Mark and bring him with you, for he is useful to me for ministry. **2 Timothy 4:11**

[10] Aristarchus my fellow prisoner greets you, with Mark the cousin of Barnabas (about whom you received instructions: if he comes to you, welcome him), **Colossians 4:10**

Philemon would have known this, therefore mentioning Mark had a virtual effect upon Philemon as well. Paul was speaking to Philemon from experience in restoration and forgiveness.

Next, there was Mr. Dependable. Dr. Luke was there attending to Paul's needs and recording the things that the Holy Spirit wanted recorded about the missionary journeys.

The most interesting person in this list is Demas. Demas had been with Paul for years now and by all accounts was a true believer. It turned out that he was an apostate and Paul was never the wiser until Demas departed and denied the faith. This tells us that age of the apostles was coming to a close as Paul was leaving people sick, including Timothy and Epahroditus, who "came close to death" without being used by the Holy Spirit to heal them. This is why we cannot determine who is a true believer and who is not. Only God truly knows who belong to Him because of the presence of the Holy Spirit who is the seal that guarantees the believers' salvation. We can only judge by their fruit, yet they could be tares. Matthew 13:37-43

Verse 25

25 The grace of our Lord Jesus Christ be with your spirit. Amen. **Philemon 1:25**

Obviously, since the letter was concerning Onesimus, Paul omitted him from this listing. However, Paul made it clear that Onesimus was a "fellow soldier" in the army of Christ (represented by Paul) to the glory of God our Father (represented by Philemon). It is all by grace through faith in Jesus sent by the love of our Heavenly Father that we are forgiven by God. Therefore, through Christ's love we should forgive others, especially within the household of faith, the body of Christ, the Church of the Living God.

This, we the true believers in Christ will do because the Spirit of Christ leads, guides, directs, and lives within us. Amen!

Prayer: What else can be said of your glorious grace, mercy, and forgiveness, O Lord God? You gave Your only begotten Son that we may have the hope of everlasting life and be reconciled to You through faith in Jesus's name. Oh, what manner of love have You bestowed upon us, that we should be made the children of God in Him? Father, I pray for those that are hurting, feeling betrayed, angry, embittered, and seeking vengeance due to some form of injustice. Look upon them Lord with mercy and grace allowing Your love, kindness, and tender mercies to empower them to lovingly forgive the people who have injured them. You know how real the pain of betrayal is, how deep the wounds created by injustice, yet You died for those who inflected these things upon You. We cry out to You, as we are numb by the reality of the pain, paralyzed by the thirst of vengeance. Forgive our weakness, O Lord. Strengthen our resolve to obey Your word, following Your example, to forgive, for our only hope and trust is in You. Now, here we stand, a forgiven rebellious former slave to sin but now a reconciled slave of righteousness to our God the Holy One of Israel, resting in the freedom of Your forgiveness in Christ Jesus the King of Glory our Savior, Master, and Lord. Thank You for helping us to overcome our bitterness, hatred, anger, malice, and thirst for vengeance, forgiving from the heart those who have injured us. Hallowed, Father, be Your name forever and ever, Amen.

BIBLIOGRAPHY

King James Version (KJV),

New King James Version (NKJV)
Publisher: Thomas Nelson
Copyright: All rights reserved
Build date: Tuesday, March 5, 2019

New International Version (NIV)
Publisher: Biblica
Copyright: © 1973, 1978, 1984, 2011 by Biblica, Inc.
Build date: Wednesday, October 23, 2019

ABOUT THE AUTHOR

Kevin Madison is an author, husband, and father who has walked faithfully with the Lord for over 30 years. He is the son of the late Pastor Leroy Phillips and Billie Mae Phillips, who raised their 13 children to love and fear the God of salvation and King of righteousness.

Modeling his study pattern after his former pastor, Carl Brown of Baton Rouge, LA, and current favorite pastors, Dr. John Barnett and Dr. John MacArthur, Kevin has become proficient at dissecting the scriptures verse by verse. Greatly impacted by his affection and love for the late Dr. J. Vernon McGee, who always challenged his listeners to study the entire word of God, Kevin has written many topical articles and yet to be published verse-by-verse commentaries on the Old Testament prophets. He is the author of several books, including *Predestined to Hell? Why would a God of Love Consign People to Hell FOREVER?*, *The Chastisement of the Lord—How the Lord Respond to Sinning Christians, America and the Judgment of Sodom & Gomorrah*, and *The God that Loves and Hates*, with several other upcoming titles soon to be published, including the much-anticipated title, *Story of the Ages—God's Plan to Eliminate the Possibility of Sin.*

www.ingramcontent.com/pod-product-compliance
Lightning Source LLC
Chambersburg PA
CBHW070437130626
46553CB00006B/2226